Flourishing in Troubling Times

Fulfilling God's Purpose
For Your Life

Bruce R. Witt

COMPASS
-finances God's way™

Flourishing in Troubling Times
Fulfilling God's Purpose for Your Life

Copyright: Bruce R. Witt 2019

Published by Compass – finances God's way – European office.

www.compass1.eu

ISBN: 978-90-830317-3-6

Flourishing in Troubling Times

Fulfilling God's Purpose For Your Life

Contents

Foreword

This book strives to help followers of Jesus to do well in difficult times in their lives, and strikes a good balance between the importance of being and doing. Being is inwardly focussed and concerns our thinking, attitudes and motivations. Doing concerns taking action. If we want to flourish in troubling times, we need to make sure that our actions flow from a right frame of mind.
Both being and doing are essential, but what we do grows out of what we are.

Shakespeare described this tension between being and doing in his play, Hamlet.
"To be, or not to be, that is the question:
Whether 'tis Nobler in the mind to suffer
The Slings and Arrows of outrageous Fortune,
Or to take Arms against a Sea of troubles....."

We can be sure that the 'arms against a sea of troubles' are the arms of Jesus Himself! It is his activity in us and through us which will help us to flourish in times of trouble.

After Jesus calmed the storm on the Sea of Galilee, he asked the disciples, "where is your faith?" He knew that the answer to flourishing in the midts of the storm was faith in Him!

In this book, Bruce helps you navigate the storms of life with both timeless principles and practical action.

Peter J. Briscoe
Former European regional director, Compass - finances God's way.

A Life Journey

We live in troubling times, from financial uncertainty to political instability, from physical war to cyber war. Every person faces struggles whether it is relational, spiritual, or physical. In spite of the gloom and doom, the bible gives us hope that not only can we survive, but we can flourish. We can thrive, grow, multiply, and bear fruit in spite of any circumstance. Our lives can be satisfying and rich in relationships and in accomplishments. How you may wonder? There is a great promise in John 16:33,

"These things I have spoken to you, so that in Me you may have peace. In the world you have tribulation, but take courage; I have overcome the world."

Christ is present to work in us and through us to give us an abundant life and experience victory.

We will outline both a spiritual journey (motivation of the heart) and practical process (strength for the hand) that will help you flourish regardless of our country, culture, job, or financial capacity. The spiritual journey is where God is transforming our hearts and relationships. The practical process, which parallels the spiritual, will guide each of us in gaining order and maturity in the use of all our resources so we can engage in God's Kingdom purposes. Each chapter will feature a story or parable of Jesus to set the stage.

There is a promise in the scriptures that combines the spiritual heart and the practical action and it relates to the handling of money.
"Instruct those who are rich in this present world not to be conceited or to fix their hope on the uncertainty of riches, but on God, who richly supplies us with all

things to enjoy. Instruct them to do good, to be rich in good works, to be generous and ready to share, storing up for themselves the treasure of a good foundation for the future, so that they may take hold of that which is life indeed." (1 Timothy 6:17).

We will map out the longer journey from challenge to hope, making application in the use of material resources so we truly will "be able take hold of life indeed."

This book will inspire the spiritual heart to go deeper with the Lord and to support our practices of being wise in use of finances. By stimulating the heart we will be able to: tackle the challenges, sustain our spiritual lives in the journey, engage in God's purpose and plan, and glorify the Lord. By strengthening the hand we will be freed up (finances and relationships in order), to do good, be generous, be rich in good works and take hold of what the Lord has in store for us.

This dual process of spiritual and practical will consider eight elements or key markers in our journey. Be encouraged as the process will be adventuresome and will truly help each of to "flourish" beyond measure.

The process has four primary stages along its path: Chaos, Order, Maturity, and Eternity. Each of these stages contains two stops in the journey.
Chaos – The Gathering Storm and a Future Hope.
Order – Surrender/Stewardship and Lifestyle Choices on Money.
Maturity – Contentment and Generosity.
Eternity – Kingdom living, resulting in Flourishing.

This book will begin to unpack both the stages and stops along this journey."

Chapter 1- Encountering the Gathering Storm

"When we long for life without difficulties, remind us that oaks grow strong in contrary winds and diamonds are made under pressure."
Peter Marshall

"We want Christ to hurry and calm the storm, He wants us to find Him in the midst of it first. No matter whose fault, God sends us through storms so we can land in a place we never would have otherwise."
Beth Moore

"Pain insists upon being attended to. God whispers to us in our pleasures, speaks in our consciences, but shouts in our pains. It is his megaphone to rouse a deaf world."
C.S. Lewis

Look around you. Depending on your vantage point you may see incredible cities and wealth, see the great good people are doing, amazing science and technology. Or you may see devastating suffering, people in poverty starving and without hope. Good and evil, joy and pain exist side by side in our lives, no matter what part of the world you call home. We often wish for a world without problems, yet it does not exist, there will always be storms to weather. We all are either in a storm, just coming out of one and getting ready to encounter one.

Today it seems that the challenges are increasing with no way out. As we consider our current times the bible indicates the road will not be easy. 2 Timothy 3:1 says "Realize this in the last days difficult times will come." We all can relate. The following parable of Jesus gives us insight on handling the storms of life.

Jesus tells us a story that will serve as a metaphor and guidance for our lives.

> *Matthew 14:22-33, "But the boat was already a long distance from the land, battered by the waves; for the wind was contrary. And in the fourth watch of the night He came to them, walking on the sea. When the disciples saw Him walking on the sea, they were terrified, and said, "It is a ghost!" And they cried out in fear. But immediately Jesus spoke to them, saying, "Take courage, it is I; do not be afraid."*
>
> *Peter said to Him, "Lord, if it is You, command me to come to You on the water." And He said, "Come!" And Peter got out of the boat, and walked on the water and came toward Jesus. But seeing the wind, he became frightened, and beginning to sink, he cried out, "Lord, save me!" Immediately Jesus stretched out His hand and took hold of him, and said to him, "You of little faith, why did you doubt?" When they got into the boat, the wind stopped. And those who were in the boat worshiped Him, saying, "You are certainly God's Son!"*

As the storm is raging, the disciples are emotional and fearful, then the Lord comes along, pursuing and inviting the disciples not to fear. The Lord is also doing the same for us in the storms we face. The question becomes what is our first response – fear and anxiousness, or is it one of faith? As we step out of the boat, do we keep eyes on the Lord or on the circumstances? If we focus on the circumstances, we will sink and the Lord will have to reach out, catch us, and guide as He did for Peter.

Wake Up to the Reality of the Day

Each day we are faced both external and internal forces in which to navigate.
The external forces are these forces that are largely beyond our control. The external forces include: the world forces of darkness and the attacks of Satan, as well as global factors such as trade wars and financial tensions. The adversities of crime, poverty, and the breakdown of the family deteriorate our communities. There is also the rapid growth in technology and globalization that quickens our pace and drive us to a greater complexity. Every country and regions has its particular political forces and national issues influence how one lives. On top of this there are physical wars and rumors of war. These challenges are increasing and will continue to be a slippery slope going forward. In short, the spiritual battle rages on, evil is taking off the mask and it will affect us all.

This is a sobering state of affairs! We must be awake and be aware of the issues of the day in order to be prepared to take action. We must not be deceived, distracted, or in denial as these forces are real.

The internal forces are just as formidable. First, there is our daily battle with the "flesh". On top of this we have a list of influences that push us toward the ditch:
Personal tensions: Rising Debt, Desiring More; Job issues, health, etc.
Financial burden – debt/bondage, no spending or saving plan, spend on self , hope in riches.
Emotional Reactions: Fear, Anxious, Bondage, Hurt, Alone, Oppressed Confusion, No Experience, no good help or answers.
Emptiness from working in our strength – trying to be God-like the first sin.
Relationships that need help and resolution.

As we acknowledge our problems, the goal is not for us to overcome them in our strength, but to realize we live in times of evil and turmoil and it will only be the Lord that can help us through it all.

Understanding the Times

In order to stand against these challenges we need to gain a new perspective by looking at our realities from God's viewpoint. This understanding brings perspective helping us see the context, the crisis, and the path forward. We need to consider what is God doing and to cultivate spiritual eyes to see Him at work. We are reminded that God speaks to us about the times in which we live.

From the following passage in Ephesians we are instructed to be careful how we walk, to watch out for the pitfalls, and be aware of the enemy who wants to push us over the edge. We need to exercise wisdom and know God's will for our daily lives. We need to use our time wisely, because, as this next verse says, these days will tempt us to follow the world's ways, and not the Lord's ways.

> *"Therefore be careful how you walk, not as unwise men but as wise, making the most of your time, because the days are evil. So then do not be foolish, but understand what the will of the Lord is. And do not get drunk with wine, for that is dissipation, but be filled with the Spirit, speaking to one another in psalms and hymns and spiritual songs, singing and making melody with your heart to the Lord; always giving thanks for all things in the name of our Lord Jesus Christ to God, even the Father."* (Ephesians 5:15-20,)

1 Chronicles 12:32, says
> *"Of the sons of Issachar, men who understood the times, with knowledge of what Israel should do."*

These verses tells us to discern the times, be a student of what is going on. Do not be uninformed or blinded. We are to have our eyes open to the reality of the days in which we live so that we exercise wisdom, not being naïve or fearful. We can't escape the evil and the challenges. We be prepared to take action.

Responding or Reacting

The bible encourages us not to react. We must be careful not to let our emotions (fear, anger, or hurt) drive us or we allow ourselves to be in denial about the times in which we live. Both paths are equally destructive.

When faced with difficulty we generally ask one of two questions "Why?" or "What?" The "Why" question is not the right question. If we are asking "Why?", it will only lead us to demand from God an answer as if we are on His level, or that we are some kind of victim. The right question to ask is "What?" What is God teaching me? What do I learn? What direction or next step do I take? There is not much difference in these questions, but where they lead us is in dramatically opposite directions. The Lord must guide us in answering these "what" questions as right answers are unique to each of us. In any and every circumstance we must seek and trust the Lord to guide as well as strengthen us to make spiritually mature responses.

Taking Action

As we encounter the storms of life we cannot sit by passively and lament that "God is in control and there is nothing one can do." We must recognize what is going on, take time to hear from the Lord, and take action. Daniel 11:32b, says,
> "...the people who know their God display strength and take action."

1 Peter 1:13, says,
> "Therefore prepare your minds For action, keep sober in spirit, fix your hope completely on the grace to be brought to you at the revelation of Jesus Christ."

We can't control the flow into our lives, yet we can control and take action with Godly attitudes, motives, and process. In order to encounter and stand up in the storm we outline eleven actions the Lord encourages us to take. They are in two overall directions: the vertical with the Lord (hearing from the Lord) and horizontal (taking action) with self and others.

Vertical Actions

Knowing God's Purposes

The Lord is not asleep at the switch. He is in charge. The Lord knows where we are and what we are going through. He does not leave us alone, nor does He withhold his unfailing love and grace in our troubles. Yet, the Lord will use trials to mold, shape, and restore us to know Him and walk with Him. He uses pain to correct us, prune us, as well as mature us, He truly has our best interests at heart. The Lord doesn't waste pain. He uses it to grow us. James 1:2-4,

> *"Consider it all joy, my brethren, when you encounter various trials, knowing that the testing of your faith produces endurance. And let endurance have its perfect result, so that you may be perfect and complete, lacking in nothing."*

Walking through the problems of life will deepen our spiritual roots and bring us to a greater intimacy with Him. We must be firm in our conviction that He promises never to leave us or forsake us.

God allows difficulties in order for us to stand out and give hope to others. We are to be a light in the darkness so that we can relate to the world and the world can relate to us, Matthew 5:16, "Let your light shine before men in such a way that they may see your good works, and glorify your Father who is in heaven." It is a process where we can minister the gospel and Christ to those in need.

> *2 Corinthians 1:3-4. "Blessed be the God and Father of our Lord Jesus Christ, the Father of mercies and God of all comfort, who comforts us in all our affliction so that we will be able to comfort those who are in any affliction with the comfort with which we ourselves are comforted by God."*

This verse is very clear, that the Lord will meet us and comfort us in our need, so that we are able to comfort others in any need. Our pain is a connection to a lost and dying world, it allows us to be real and authentic in our struggles. This is actually attractive to people in need and will cause the lost to ask what makes us different.

Hearing God's Message

We began the quote from C.S. Lewis "God shouts in our pains. It is his megaphone to rouse a deaf world." The Lord uses our pain for a purpose, as we saw above he uses it to mold and correct us,

He also uses it to speak to our hearts when we are in need. Jesus speaks to this in John 7:37-38,

> *"Jesus stood and cried out, saying, "If anyone is thirsty, let him come to Me and drink. He who believes in Me, as the Scripture said, 'From his innermost being will flow rivers of living water."*

We see the Lord reaching out to the thirsty - those who need the Lord and His presence. God is calling and inviting. Are we listening? Are we taking note?

As you encounter problems, stop what you are doing! Step back from the challenge and begin to take note of what is the message God is trying to speak to your heart.

Hearing leads to biblical action. God calls to us and wants to prepare us for troubling times ahead.

> *"Therefore everyone who hears these words of Mine and acts on them, may be compared to a wise man who built his house on the rock. And the rain fell, and the floods came, and the winds blew and slammed against that house; and yet it did not fall, for it had been founded on the rock. Everyone who hears these words of Mine and does not act on them, will be like a foolish man who built his house on the sand. The rain fell, and the floods came, and the winds blew and slammed against that house; and it fell—and great was its fall." (Matthew 7:24-27)*
> *Which rock are you building on?*

Thanking the Lord

We are called to thank the Lord in everything. Note the following verses on thankfulness, there is no condition as to how good or bad the circumstances. We are to thank the Lord continually.

> *"Be anxious for nothing, but in everything by prayer and supplication with thanksgiving let your requests be made known to God." (Philippians 4:6)*

> *"In everything give thanks; for this is God's will for you in Christ Jesus." (1 Thessalonians 5:18)*

Thanking the Lord is one of the first steps we should take. We will receive a great blessing in doing so.

Horizontal Actions

Journeying on Life's Road

Life is not easy, it is demanding and at times arduous. This life and our spiritual walk could best be described as a journey that we are traveling. It is a process with many turns, twists, and choices.

This trip has a final destination of an eternal home for all of us. Too often we are caught up in the busyness of the moment and don't see the big picture of following Christ and learning life lessons along the way. This adventure in life will contain many unknowns and it will take more than a formula or a set of techniques to navigate the road. One needs a relationship with the guide who knows the way. The Lord in His grace and mercy will both direct us and fill us with a sense of His presence.

Ken Boa, in Conformed to His Image, has a great observation about the process. "Seen in this light, the primary point of this earthly existence is preparation for our eternal citizenship in heaven. It is to learn to respond to God's providential care in deepening ways and to accept the pilgrim character of earthly existence with its uncertainties, setbacks, disappointments, surprises, and joys. It is to remember that we are in a process of gradual conformity to the image of Christ so that we can love and serve others along the way.

In this life we stumble in many ways (James 3:2) because we are still in process—our sanctification is not yet complete.
This journey is not a submission to a set of legalistic do's and don'ts rather it is a response to God's invitation to be a part of His family, so we may be growing, learning, and enjoying life from Him. The blessing is that we experience Him in both the journey and forever in the destination. When we seek God's purpose's we have eternal life and He throws in the enjoyment of the process.

Embracing the Pain

Paul reminds these believers that the conflict and pain they saw in him, they too must accept and endure. This would not be an option but a certainty. We all need to be reminded of this. Pain will come if we follow Christ, yet be encouraged because it has many redeeming qualities.

"For to you it has been granted for Christ's sake, not only to believe in Him, but also to suffer for His sake, experiencing the same conflict which you saw in me, and now hear to be in me."
(Philippians 1:29-30)

C.S. Lewis inhis book, The Problem of Pain, says "when pain is to be born, a little courage helps more than much knowledge, a little human sympathy more than much courage, and the least tincture of the love of God more than all."

As we approach the problem of pain, we make several observations:
1. Pain, difficulties, and struggles have existed since Adam & Eve and will not cease until Christ returns.
2. Pain has its origin in evil and/or sin. We live in a world where ALL IS NOT WELL.
3. Every person experiences pain – it is universal. We all may not have happiness, we all will have pain.
4. Pain can be a warning signal of our limits, it highlights when we are approaching a problem.
5. Pain can be redemptive if seen from God's view. There are a number of blessings with pain.

Jesus was honest about pain. He told us the truth. He said in John 16:33,

"You will have suffering in this world."
He didn't say you might – he said it is going to happen.

Part of the challenge with pain is that we don't see with God's eyes. 1 Corinthians 13:12 says,

"Now we see things imperfectly, like puzzling reflections in a mirror, but then we will see everything with perfect clarity. All that I know now is partial and in-

complete, but then I will know everything completely, just as God now knows me completely."

Lee Strobel offers us a reflection on pain and suffering that he calls "Five Points of Light."

The first point of light: God is not the creator of evil and suffering.
God did not create evil and suffering. Now, it's true that he did create the potential for evil to enter the world, because that was the only way to create the potential for genuine goodness and love. But it was human beings, in our free will, who brought that potential evil into reality.

The second point of light is this: Though suffering isn't good, God can use it to accomplish good.

He does this by fulfilling His promise in Romans 8:28:
"And we know that in all things God works for the good of those who love him, who have been called according to his purpose."

Notice that the verse doesn't say God causes evil and suffering, just that he promises to cause good to emerge. God can use our suffering to draw us to Himself, to mold and sharpen our character, to influence others for Him – He can draw something good from our pain in a myriad of ways...if we trust and follow Him.

The third point of light: The day is coming when suffering will cease and God will judge evil.

God is actually delaying the consummation of history in anticipation that some of you will still put your trust in Him and spend eternity in heaven. He's delaying everything out of His love for you. 2 Peter 3:9 says:
"The Lord is not slow in keeping His promise, as some understand slowness. He is patient with you, not wanting anyone to perish, but everyone to come to repentance."
To me, that's evidence of a loving God, that He would care that much for you.

Point of Light #4: Our suffering will pale in comparison to what God has in store for his followers.

God promises a time when there will be no more crying, no more tears, no more pain and suffering, when we will be reunited with God in perfect harmony, forever. Let the words of First Corinthians 2:9 soak into your soul: "No eye has seen, no ear has heard, no mind has conceived what God has prepared for those who love him." That's absolutely breath-taking, isn't it?

Point of Light #5: We decide whether to turn bitter or turn to God for peace and courage.
God offers us the two very things we need when we're hurting: peace to deal with our present and courage to deal with our future. How? Because he has conquered the world! Through His own suffering and death, He has deprived this world of its ultimate power over you. Suffering doesn't have the last word anymore. Death doesn't have the last word anymore. God has the last word!

Our application could be to reflect how God has used your suffering to shape and grow you. Share this with another. Don't go alone, Focusing on your pain will isolate you and can take you out of the journey. Don't live in denial. From the depths of a Nazi death camp, Corrie ten Boom wrote these words: "No matter how deep our darkness, He is deeper still. Every tear we shed becomes his tear."

Engaging in The Warfare

As followers of Christ, we are involved in an all-encompassing conflict, whether we know it or not. Scripture clearly teaches and illustrates the dynamics of this warfare on the three battlefronts of the world, the flesh, and the devil. The worldly and demonic systems are external to believers, but they entice and provide opportunities for the flesh, which is the capacity for sin within us. Christ has already won the victory, but until He returns, the battle still rages on three fronts: the world, the flesh, and the devil (Ephesians 2:2-3).

1. **The world.** "In the world you have tribulation, but take courage; I have overcome the world" (John 16:33b). "For whatever

is born of God overcomes the world; and this is the victory that has overcome the world—our faith" (1 John 5:4).

2. **The flesh**. "But I say, walk by the Spirit, and you will not carry out the desire of the flesh. For the flesh sets its desire against the Spirit, and the Spirit against the flesh; for these are in opposition to one another, so that you may not do the things that you please" (Galatians 5:16-17).

3. **The devil**. ". . . the ruler of this world has been judged" (John 16:11b). ". . . the word of God abides in you, and you have overcome the evil one. . . . greater is He who is in you than he who is in the world" (1 John 2:14b; 4:4b).

Note the description of the battle in the book of Ephesians,

"Finally, be strong in the Lord and in the strength
of His might. Put on the full armor of God, that you
will be able to stand firm against the schemes of the
devil. For our struggle is not against flesh and blood,
but against the rulers, against the powers, against
the world forces of this darkness, against the spiritual
forces of wickedness in the heavenly places. There-
fore, take up the full armor of God, so that you will be
able to resist in the evil day, and having done every-
thing, to stand firm" (Ephesians 6:10-13).

The New Testament exhorts us to realize that a war is going on, to recognize the strategies of the enemy, and to know how to fight. It is important that we maintain a biblical balance as we consider the warfare.

"There are two equal and opposite errors into which our race can fall about the devils. One is to disbelieve in their existence. The other is to believe, and to feel an excessive and unhealthy interest in them. They themselves are equally pleased by both errors" (C. S. Lewis, Preface to The Screwtape Letters).

Those who ignore the biblical teaching about the reality of the enemy and the weapons of the warfare put themselves in a dangerous position of vulnerability.

"For though we walk in the flesh, we do not war according to the flesh, for the weapons of our warfare are not of the flesh, but divinely powerful for the destruction for fortresses" (2 Corinthians 10:3-4).

The spiritual warfare is an everyday process; sometimes we are aware of and sometimes not. As we seek and follow the Lord the target on our back grows and we are not only participating in the battle we become the focus of the enemies wrath. We never have enough strength or wisdom to combat the enemy in ourselves, thus we need an intimate walk with the Lord to unleash His power to fight through us.

Paul exhorts us to "put on the full armor of God" so that we can "stand firm against the schemes of the devil" (Ephesians 6:11). This metaphor makes it clear that the spiritual warfare is pro-active; we must be prepared, ready to resist, and empowered to advance into enemy territory. Christ is the Victor who calls us to stand on the ground He has won through His blood. As long as we are prepared for battle, we need not retreat before any intruder. It is wise to pray on the armor of God each morning, because without it we are open to attack." Ken Boa

Believing in God's Promises

Take some time to be quiet and reflect on what God promises to each of us. These are especially encouraging when we are in a struggle or battle. These promises are a firm foundation for the working out of our faith. These are blessings we receive in our brokenness.

Deuteronomy 32:10,11	God watches over us and shields us in the difficulties.
Psalms 9:9,10	God is a refuge and a stronghold in times of trouble.
Psalms 46:1-3	God is a safe place and will help us when we need it.
Psalms 147:3	God heals up the brokenhearted and binds up the wounded.
Isaiah 41:10	God will uphold as we wait upon the Lord.
Lamentations 3:19-26, 33	God's love and compassion are new and never fail.

Romans 6:5	We are untied with Him in death and we will be united in his life.
Romans 8:18	Affliction is momentary and light in comparison to the glory we will receive.
Romans 8:28	God works all things for good according to his riches in Glory.
1 Corinthians 10:13	God will make a way through the valley, a way of escape in temptation.
2 Corinthians 1:3-7	God comforts us out of His character.
2 Corinthians 4:16-18	God renews us in our difficulties. We receive have an eternal weight of glory.
Philippians 4:13	We can do all things through Christ who strengthens us.
Hebrews 4:15, 16	Christ has been through suffering and He will give us mercy and grace.
1 Peter 5:7	Cast all your cares upon him because he cares for you.

Connecting with One Another

The one thing we must watch out for is not to become isolated. This is exactly where the enemy wants us to be. If we are alone in our challenges and pain, the problem magnifies and our emotions give us false signals. We need one another, God does not call us or expect us to go through the pain by ourselves. The following quotes give us a clear understanding about the value of connecting with others.

Larry Crabb - "Beneath all our problems there are desperately hurting souls that must find the nourishment only community can provide or die. The greatest need in modern civilization is the development of communities - true communities where the heart of God is home, where the humble and wise learn to shepherd those on the path behind them, where trusting strugglers lock arms with others as together they journey on."

G. K. Chesteron "the man who lives in a small community lives in a much larger world... The reason is obvious. In a large community we can choose our companions. In a small community our companions are chosen for us. Community is the place where the person you least want to live with always lives. Often we surround ourselves with the people we most want to live with, thus forming a club or clique, not a community. Anyone can form a club, it takes grace, shared vision and hard work to form a community.

Henri Nouwen " Nothing is sweet or easy about community. Community is a fellowship of people who do not hide their joys and sorrows but make them visible to each other in a gesture of hope. In community we say: Life is full of gains and losses, joys and sorrows, ups and downs - but we do not have to live it alone. We want to drink our cup together and thus celebrate the truth that the wounds of our individual lives, which seem intolerable when live alone, become sources of healing when we live them as part of a fellowship of mutual care."

Making Practical Choices

As we walk through the storms of life, our handling of money and resources is a clear picture into our spiritual heart. How we handle money and what we think of it is like a thermometer that measures the degree of your fever, handling money measures our spiritual heart. The most direct question we can ask ourselves that will reflect our hearts is "How much is enough?" The big problem for those who cannot answer "The question how much is Enough?" is that they are constantly being bombarded by new needs both internally from our own desires far more externally by television and magazines language advertisements tempting us to want even more and more. This leads to unrest and the constant feeling that we do not have enough and that we continually need new things for a fulfilled life. Epicurus, the Greek philosopher, said, "Nothing is enough for the man to whom enough is too little"

Dr. Thomas Sedlacek says, in his book "The Economics of Good and Evil," "The more we have, the more we want. Why? Perhaps we thought (and this sounds truly intuitive) that the more we have, the less we will need. We thought that consumption leads to saturation of our needs. But the opposite has proven to be true. The more we have, the more additional things we need. Every new satisfied want will beget a new one and will leave us wanting. For consumption is like a drug." It is said that an illness of our common times is affluenza. Answering the question of 'how much is enough' will cure the prevailing sickness of 'affluenza'...

Prof. Dr. E.F. Schumacher, author of the seminal work "Small is Beautiful" says that foolishness is the cultivation and expansion of needs. These do not lead to freedom and peace. He further says that increasing needs make us vulnerable to outside forces over which we have no control and this increases the fear factor that we will never have enough. He goes on to say that the only way in which we can reduce this fear factor which leads to stress in life is the reduction of needs. Therefore, we have to examine our life very carefully and determine what we really need. This is answering the question "how much is enough?".

How Much Land Does a Man Need?   Leo Tolstoy

To illustrate "How much is enough?" Leo Tolstoy tells the story of a greedy man named, Pahom, who was obsessed by amassing more and more land. Pahom hears a rumor about the land of the Bashkirs. There, a tradesman tells him, a man can obtain land for less than a penny an acre, simply by making friends with the chiefs. Fueled by the desire for more, cheaper, and better land, Pahom seeks directions for the land of the Bashkirs and leaves on a journey to obtain the land that he thinks he needs. On arrival, he distributes gifts to the Bashkir leaders and finds them courteous and friendly. He explains his reasons for being there and, after some deliberation, they offer him whatever land he wants for one thousand rubles. Pahom is pleased but concerned; he wants boundaries, deeds, and "official sanction" to give him the assurance he needs that they or their children will never reverse their decision.

The Bashkirs agree to this arrangement, and a deal is struck. Pahom can have all the land that he can walk around in a day for one thousand rubles. The one condition is that if he does not return on the same day to the spot at which he began, the money will be lost. The night before his fateful walk, Pahom plans his strategy; he will try to encircle thirty-five miles of land and then sell the poorer land to peasants at a profit. When he awakes the next day, he is met by the man whom he thought was the chief of the Bash-kirs, but whom he recognizes as the peasant who had come to his old home to tell him of lucrative land deals available elsewhere. He looks again, and realizes that he is speaking with the devil himself. He dismisses this meeting as merely a dream and goes about his walk.

Pahom starts well, but he tries to encircle too much land, and by midday he realizes that he has tried to create too big a circuit. Though afraid of death, he knows that his only chance is to complete the circuit. "There is plenty of land," he says to himself, "but will God let me live on it?" As the sun comes down, Pahom runs with all his remaining strength to the spot where he began. Reaching it, he sees the chief laughing and holding his sides; he remembers his dream and breathes his last breath. Pahom's servant picks up the spade with which Pahom had been marking his land and digs a grave in which to bury him: "Six feet from his head to his heels was all he needed."

Applying God's Word

We don't have the power to change our stories of brokenness and hurt, the only way to change our story is to embed it in God's story. He can and will transform us in order to make something new and wonderful from our broken lives.

Start with examining your heart.
Be ready to modify how you use money, this is God's means to grow us and reveal to us where our hearts truly lie.
Move out of chaos to order through the process of correction, instruction, and obedience.
Submit to the Lord's direction in finances.
Seek the Lord in the challenges, call and pray to Him.
Be Encouraged - You are not alone.
Start thanking Him in every situation.
Help others in greater need. It helps us moves eye off of our self or our challenging circumstances.
Begin to a personal spiritual growth plan to keeping and to prepare for difficult days ahead.

Find an accountability partner to ask you the tough questions.

Do a personal assessment.

Find someone who is going through difficult time (maybe more than yourself) and minister to them personally and practically.

A short summary and challenge for us is to see where we are (gain perspective), to reflect and observe our next steps, take action by serving the Lord and others all the while we are pressing into Him and pressing on to His mission.

Assessing Yourself

How are you doing in your growth and maturity? We must set back and consider there are seven absolutes to living well. The first and most important question: is Christ at the center of our lives? This is followed by six factors that revolve around this. The opportunity is to keep growing in each of these areas and not be too weighted in any one or two areas while overlooking other areas. Each of these seven are important in our journey, and they are captured by roles that we play.

"I do all things for the sake of the gospel, so that I may become a fellow partaker of it. Do you not know that those who run in a race all run, but only one receives the prize? Run in such a way that you may win. Everyone who competes in the games, exercises self-control in all things. They then do it to receive a perishable wreath, but we an imperishable. Therefore I run in such a way, as not without aim; I box in such a way, as not beating the air; but I discipline my body and make it my slave, so that, after I have preached to others, I myself will not be disqualified." (1 Corinthians 9:23-27)

"But I do not consider my life of any account as dear to myself, so that I may finish my course and the ministry which I received from the Lord Jesus, to testify solemnly of the gospel of the grace of God." (Acts 20:24)

1. Keep Jesus and the Gospel central in order to live as Christ
   and seek His eternal Kingdom. Christ is the Christian life lived
   out through us, and apart from Him we can do nothing. In
   this, we are called to be a **FOLLOWER**. We follow Christ and
   His teachings. It is not about us or our agendas, it is all about
   God's Kingdom purposes.
   Look up: Philippians 1:21, 1 Corinthians 9:23, Psalms 73:28

2. Bring order to our Money and Finances to lay a foundation for
   freedom and peace. Without a sense of order, we will be in
   chaos or consumed by money and our attitudes towards money. We tend to think money is life unless we come to a place
   of knowing it is the Lord's, and we are simply a **STEWARD**.
   We are managers of God's resources and will have to give an
   account of them. Being a steward frees us up and allows us a
   better perspective.
   Look up: 1 Chronicles 29:11-12, 1 Corinthians 4:2, Matthew
   6:19-21

3. Clarify why you go to Work and what your Purpose is in order
   to produce direction and priorities. We are called to work and
   commanded to provide for the needs of our families. Work is
   important but should not consume us or define who we are.
   When we clarify the purpose of our lives, work then will take
   its proper place and become a context to live out God's purposes from which we play the role of **SERVANT**. We are called to
   serve others and put them ahead of ourselves.
   Look up: Matthew 5:16, Colossians 3:3, Colossians 1:27-29

4. Define true Success and Significance to empower our motivation and refine our motives.
   In order to have balance and perspective, a Biblical view of
   success and significance is critical. Success from God's viewpoint is to glorify Him, serve others, obey His teachings, and
   bear fruit of love, joy, peace, etc. When we see life through the
   innocence of a **CHILD**, this will keep us from thinking too
   highly of ourselves and of our work. We become more centered
   on God and others. Seeing others succeed and rejoicing with
   them brings us as well as the Lord great joy. Look up: 2 Corinthians 5:17, Matthew 6:33, 1 Corinthians 6:20

5. Value Relationships and Community with love to create whole-
    ness and give meaning to life.
    God created this world and people were His highest creation.
    He made us in His image and not even angels have this distinc-
    tion. We are called to love others, and give our lives to them.
    We also realize that none of us have all of the gifts or talents so
    we need one another. One role we play in relation with oth-
    ers is to be a **SHEPHERD**, one who cares for, who oversees
    the needs and protection of others. This does not lift us above
    anyone else, it brings us into a giving relationship for the good
    of others.
    Look up: 1 Thessalonians 2:8, 1 Corinthians 12:12, Romans
    12:10

6. Respond appropriately to life's Circumstances and Challenges
    because it will build or break you.
    Probably one the greatest challenges we have as Christians is
    to think and respond appropriately when life throws us a curve
    ball of pain, hurt, difficulty, or closed doors. Having a right
    perspective of these is critical, or we may focus too much on
    the losses, become upset with the Lord, frustrated with others,
    feel worthless, or want to get even. We live in a fallen world,
    and we must see life from God's viewpoint. It will not be easy.
    When we see ourselves as a **SLAVE** of Christ then our expec-
    tations are recalibrated. We see life from God's standpoint. We
    recognize that life is not about ourselves, what we deserve, or
    what we are entitled to. We rest in the fact God is still in con-
    trol and from this place, we can even thank Him.
    Look up: 2 Corinthians 4:7-11, Isaiah 1:2-4, Romans 8:28

7. Handle your Resources with Generosity in order to bless oth-
    ers and reap an eternal reward. The Lord gives us many things:
    finances, talents, gifts, abilities, and relationships just to name
    a few. The question is not based on what have we been given?
    Rather, it is what did we do with what we have been given?
    Do we hoard these resources for our selfish use, or do we have
    an attitude of generosity by giving to the Lord and others?
    We play the role of **FRIEND** when we put others ahead of
    ourselves. This honors the Lord, and He promises to bless us
    when we do.

Look up: 2 Corinthians 9:6-7, 1 Peter 4:10, Proverbs 11:35

In each of these seven areas, rate your self on a scale of 1-10 on how well you are doing. Write out some specific steps that will help you to grow and maintain your balance. The big idea is to use these to examine where we are in these areas, where we have a blind spot, and where we to need to grow. This is not a list of to-do's, they are arenas of life where one needs to grow and mature.

This is a process will take time to move to a place of maturity. This is the goal of our walk with the Lord, Ephesians 4:13, "until we all attain to the unity of the faith, and of the knowledge of the Son of God, to a mature man, to the measure of the stature which belongs to the fullness of Christ."

Exercise

On a scale of 1-10 rate yourself in each of the seven areas:

1. _____ Keep Jesus and the Gospel central in order to live as Christ and seek the eternal Kingdom.

2. _____ Bring order to your Money and Finances to lay a foundation for freedom and peace.

3. _____ Clarify why you go to Work and what your Purpose is in order to produce direction and priorities.

4. _____ Define true Success and Significance to empower your motivation and refine your motives.

5. _____ Value Relationships and Community with love to create wholeness and give meaning to life.

6. _____ Respond appropriately to life's Circumstances and Challenges because it will build or break you.

7. _____ Handle your Resources with Generosity in order to bless others and reap an eternal reward.

Chapter 2 –
Finding Hope in the Midst of the Trials

"To live without Hope is to cease to live."
Fyodor Dostoevsky

"You define life backwards and then live it forward,"
Soren Kierkegaard

A Christian reflection on pain must end with a vision of heaven, the true end and home of humanity. Citing Paul, C.S. Lewis contrasts the "suffering of the present time" with the glory of heaven; but he insists that heaven is not a bribe, for it "offers nothing that a mercenary soul could desire. It is safe to tell the pure in heart that they shall see God, for only the pure in heart want to"(!). Lewis makes us desire heaven; he even claims that, in our heart of hearts, we have never desired anything else. "God will look to every soul like its first love because He is its first love". And every soul is unique: "Your place in heaven will seem to be made for you alone, because you were made for it."

Finding and living with hope is probably the greatest spiritual activity and discipline we can exercise. Hope motivates us, focuses our attention on the Lord and His character rather than on our circumstances. Hope offers perspective to make wise choices in order to journey on with a positive attitude versus being angry and bitter. Hope grows our faith and love so that others grow.

When we face the trials and storms of life and are being rocked by the winds and waves, what do we do? The storm is literally a spiritual battle of good and evil. We saw previously in Matthew 14 when Peter responded to Jesus' call to come in the midst of the storm, he began well, his eyes and perspective were on Jesus Christ.

When he shifted his perspective to the waves and the circumstances, he began to sink. When we face the challenges and heartaches of life where is our focus? We can look around and be filled with fear and anxiousness or look to Christ, our true hope, and walk on top of the waves rather than being overcome by them. What is your perspective in the struggles? Where is your hope?

Jesus tells a story of the ten virgins which is a clear picture of hope, of being ready and prepared to meet the Christ.

> *"Then the kingdom of heaven will be comparable to ten virgins, who took their lamps and went out to meet the bridegroom. Five of them were foolish, and five were prudent. For when the foolish took their lamps, they took no oil with them, but the prudent took oil in flasks along with their lamps.*
> *Now while the bridegroom was delaying, they all got drowsy and began to sleep. But at midnight there was a shout, 'Behold, the bridegroom! Come out to meet him.' Then all those virgins rose and trimmed their lamps. The foolish said to the prudent, 'Give us some of your oil, for our lamps are going out.' But the prudent answered, 'No, there will not be enough for us and you too; go instead to the dealers and buy some for yourselves.' And while they were going away to make the purchase, the bridegroom came, and those who were ready went in with him to the wedding feast; and the door was shut. Later the other virgins also came, saying, 'Lord, lord, open up for us.' But he answered, 'Truly I say to you, I do not know you.' Be on the alert then, for you do not know the day nor the hour."* (Matthew 25:1-13,)

Five virgins were looking forward with a hope and certainty of Christ's return, they took the time and cost to prepare, they were focused. Five virgins were foolish in that they allowed the things and the cares of daily living distract them and lose focus. Hope gives us this sense of what is important and being alert.

A biblical "hope" is that of certainty based on God's immutable character. There is an assurance as to the result – it is a fact. Hope is the reason for our faith, for our life. Hope is tied to a person, object, or idea. We will see that this hope is reflected tangibly in how we handle our finances and motivates us to a lifestyle of contentment, generosity, and investing in eternity.

> *"Instruct those who are rich in this present world)
> not to be conceited or to fix their hope on the uncertainty of riches, but on God, who richly supplies us
> with all things to enjoy. Instruct them to do good, to
> be rich in good works, to be generous and ready to
> share, storing up for themselves the treasure of a good
> foundation for the future, so that they may take hold
> of that which is life indeed." (1 Timothy 6:17)*

"To flourish in troubling times" we first must be real about our circumstances, not living in denial or consumed by them. Next, we must establish a biblical hope that will motivate and sustain us to persevere. A true biblical hope will motivate us through our temporal life filled with its problems because the focus is eternal. The author Soren Kierkegaard said, "One never really lives unless he has something to die for." We must have a cause or goal in life that transcends the daily grind and the ongoing pursuit of getting ahead. If we have a reason for living, it will motivate us to persevere in our spiritual walk. Hope sets a foundation for the purpose of our lives. When we are clear about "why" we are here, we can tackle almost any "what or how."

The quality of your life now and your life in eternity is primarily determined by your hope. Hope involves answering 'why' we are here. It helps us determine what are our motivations, guides us in setting direction and live out our priorities. What gives you passion, excitement, what inspires you? Ephesians 1:18-19 describes the hope of our calling, what we are giving our life to.

"I pray that the eyes of your heart may be enlightened, so that you will know what is the hope of His calling, what are the riches of the

glory of His inheritance in the saints, and what is the surpassing greatness of His power toward us who believe."
These are in accordance with the working of the strength of His might."

What is Hope?

The world considers hope wishful thinking, a feeling that what is wanted can be had or that events will turn out for the best: to give up hope. a particular instance of this feeling: the hope of winning. a person or thing in which expectations are centered: The medicine was her last hope. Archaic. to place trust; rely. Most people have a real misconception of what hope is. They define hope from a temporary or worldly view – "I 'hope' this situation turns out like I want."

Hope is a confident assurance. Hope is the reason for our faith, for our life. Paul in his letter to the Colossians said that the Spirit of Jesus Christ in each believer is our hope.

> "To them God has chosen to make known among the Gentiles the glorious riches of this mystery, which is Christ in you, the hope of glory." (Colossians 1:27)

We have the hope of life and eternity in us! This becomes the source of giving and serving others with the generosity that Christ has extended to us.

Start with a Fresh Perspective – Seeing From God's Viewpoint

How we see things will help us move forward or be stuck. Do we see our difficulties as challenges or opportunities? My 'hope' will influence my viewpoint. Isaiah 51:6, encourages us to look up,
> "Lift up your eyes to the sky, then look to the earth beneath; for the sky will vanish like smoke, and the earth will wear out like a garment and its inhabitants will die in like manner; but My salvation will be forever, and My righteousness will not wane."

Where was Jesus' hope when faced with the impossibility of feeding the thousands with almost no resources? He did two things: He looked up and He gave thanks.

> *"And He took the five loaves and the two fish, and looking up toward heaven, He blessed the food and broke the loaves and He kept giving them to the disciples to set before them; and He divided up the two fish among them all."* (Mark 6:41)

Seeing from God's perspective directs our attention to rise above the circumstances, seeing the both the horizon and see the Lord at work. There is a promise in Psalms 139:5 that He goes before us, comes after us, and walks with us so we are not alone. In addition, with hope we see the end, we see the final scenes of the play and we know that the victory belongs to the Lord. We see our hope being realized and thus our actions in the moment can be one of confidence and peace.

The Source of Hope – God's Character, His Plan, and His Son

God's character is the ultimate source of our hope! He is unchanging, always loving, all-knowing, and all-powerful as we see in Psalms 139. This becomes the rock upon which we can build our lives and our future which is same rock Jesus described on the Sermon on the Mount.

In addition to character, God has a plan for this world and a purpose for our lives. This plan and purpose is articulated in the promise God has for His people in Jeremiah 29:11-14;

> *"For I know the plans that I have for you,' declares the Lord, 'plans for welfare and not for calamity to give you a future and a hope. Then you will call upon Me and come and pray to Me, and I will listen to you. You will seek Me and find Me when you search for Me with all your heart. I will be found by you,' declares the Lord, 'and I will restore your fortunes and will gather you from all the nations and from all the places where I have driven you,"*

Hope is not found in this world or the things of this world, its origin is solely in God the Father and the Lord Jesus Christ. We need to truly know God the Father and Jesus at a heart level in order to appropriate and experience this hope.

Hope is the Motivation for My Faith

Much of our Christian teaching about living life centers on our faith and rightfully so. We have our faith in Christ who provided the salvation of our sins. Faith defines our actions and how we live.

Where does faith comes from? Faith is a product of HOPE.
"Faith is the assurance of things hoped for and the convictions of things not seen." (Hebrews 11:1)

If you want to grow your faith, grow your hope. This comes as we gain a larger view of God, His character and the love which He showers upon us. Hope grows as we recognize the infinite amount of grace that has been given to you and further consider that you deserved none of it.

Hope spurs us to action and to exercise faith. People move in the direction of what they believe to be gain. We invest where we think there will be a return. We all want to invest in what will last. The scriptures are clear that there are only two things that will last – people and the Word of God. These are what we need to spend our time, talent, and treasure on.
"For who is our hope or joy or crown of exultation? Is it not even you, in the presence of our Lord Jesus at His coming?" (1 Thessalonians 2:19)

Are people your priority? How about God's Word?

Viktor Frankl, having survived the brutality and horror of the Nazi concentration camps, wrote a book "Man's Search for Meaning." He makes that following observations.
"It is a peculiarity of man that he can only live by looking to the future. And this is his salvation in the most difficult moments of his existence, although he sometimes has to force his mind to the task.

I remember a personal experience. Almost in tears from pain (I had terrible sores on my feet from wearing torn shoes), I limped a few kilometers with our long column of men from the camp to our work site. Very cold, bitter winds struck us. I kept thinking of the endless little problems of our miserable life. What would there be to eat tonight? If a piece of sausage came as extra ration, should I exchange it for a piece of bread? Should I trade my last cigarette, which was left from a bonus I received a fortnight ago, for a bowl of soup? How could I get a piece of wire to replace the fragment which served as one of my shoelaces?

I became disgusted with the state of affairs which compelled me, daily and hourly, to think of only such trivial things. I forced my thoughts to turn to another subject. Suddenly I saw myself standing on the platform of a well-lit, warm and pleasant lecture room. In front of me sat an attentive audience on comfortable upholstered seats. I was giving a lecture on the psychology of the concentration camp! All that oppressed me at that moment became objective, seen and described from the remote viewpoint of science. By this method I succeeded somehow in rising above the situation, above the sufferings of the moment, and I observed them as if they were already of the past.

The prisoner who had lost faith in the future - his future - was doomed. With his loss of belief in the future, he also lost his spiritual hold; he let himself decline and became subject to mental and physical decay."

The core of this process of finding and living God's purpose for your life is found in capturing from the Lord His vision and purpose for your life and how it intersects with His greater plan. This purpose directs our steps today and gives us a future hope for tomorrow. A perspective of hope is what motivates us.

Hope in Difficulty

Hope and difficulty go hand in hand. Let us consider three aspects of how hope is helpful in our challenges.

Hope is an Anchor of the Soul.

Hope is the anchor for us in the storm. It holds us secure and solid.

> *"In the same way God, desiring even more to show to the heirs of the promise the unchangeableness of His purpose, interposed with an oath, so that by two unchangeable things in which it is impossible for God to lie, we who have taken refuge would have strong encouragement to take hold of the hope set before us. This hope we have as an anchor of the soul, a hope both sure and steadfast and one which enters within the veil, 20 where Jesus has entered as a forerunner for us..." (Hebrews 6:17-20)*

Hope is Clarified in the Difficulties.

Hope is clarified in the times of the difficulty to sustain me in the times of the good. When the problems surround us we realize that not all things are important, truly only a few things are most critical. If one has a dying friend or is battling cancer, if my favorite sports team wins or loses is not so important. Thus we realize that the difficulties help order our priorities and life form a place of Christ-centeredness.

> *"We also exult in our tribulations, knowing that tribulation brings about perseverance; and perseverance proven character; and proven character, hope; and hope does not disappoint." (Romans 5:3-5)*

Afflictions Help Develop our Ministry.

We see that God meets us and comforts us in our afflictions so we will be empathic and have an increased heart to minister to others in need.

> *"Blessed be the God and Father of our Lord Jesus Christ, the Father of mercies and God of all comfort, who comforts us in all our affliction so that we will be able to comfort those who are in any affliction with the comfort with which we ourselves are comforted by God. For just as the sufferings of Christ are ours in abundance, so also our comfort is abundant through Christ." (2 Corinthians 1:3-5)*

People relate to us more in our pain than they do in our victories. We become real to them, Christians have the same struggles as the lost world they just have a different hope. Pain is a gift of God so we can offer hope to others.

Life is lived in the valleys and you are going to get through them. The temptation is to withdraw and hide.

Four Types of Hope

There are four types of hope.
- True and better hope – Hope in Christ
- Wrong hope – lost people pursuing fame, riches, power.
- Misplaced – wrong motives – saved people with a foot in two worlds. Double minded
- No hope – people in true despair.

We need to examine ourselves and see where our hearts are in relation to what kind of hope defines our lives. Otherwise we will confuse needs, wants, desires, and hope.

"Our Lord finds our desires, not too strong, but too weak. We are half-hearted creatures, fooling about with drink and sex and ambition when infinite joy is offered us, like an ignorant child who wants to go on making mud pies in a slum because he cannot imagine what is meant by the offer of a holiday at the sea. We are far too easily pleased."
C.S. Lewis, The Weight of Glory

Where is your Hope? Beyond our hope in Christ, our hope should center on people, heaven, the gospel and the word.

"For who is our hope or joy or crown of exultation? Is it not even you, in the presence of our Lord Jesus at His coming? For you are our glory and joy." (1 Thessalonians 2:19-20)

"...because of the hope laid up for you in heaven, of which you previously heard in the word of truth, the gospel..." (Colossians 1:5)

"...if indeed you continue in the faith firmly established and steadfast, and not moved away from the hope of the gospel that you have heard, which was proclaimed in all creation under heaven, and of which I, Paul, was made a minister." (Colossians 1:23)

"For whatever was written in earlier times was written for our instruction, so that through perseverance and the encouragement of the Scriptures we might have hope." (Romans 15:4)

The Hope of Christ in you – Experiencing the Abundant Life

On many occasions the Bible describes that Christ is our life. If Christ is our life, this is much more than being Christ-like. To be Christ-like is to look like Christ in our actions, and attitudes. To have Christ as our life is to realize He lives in us in the form of the Spirit and we take on His strength, His power, and His wisdom. Take note of the following verses and consider what they say about the source and substance of our life. This is what Paul was saying that for him to live is Christ, (Christ working in and through him). This is radically different from trying hard to imitate Christ or to do what Christ did in our own strength.

"For to me, to live is Christ, and to die is gain." (Philippians 1:21)

"I have been crucified with Christ; and it is no longer I who live, but Christ lives in me; and the life which I now live in the flesh I live by faith in the Son of God, who loved me and gave Himself up for me." (Galatians 2:20)

"The thief comes only to steal and kill and destroy; I came that they may have life, and have it abundantly." (John 10:10)

"For you have died and your life is hidden with Christ in God. When Christ, who is our life, is revealed, then

you also will be revealed with Him in glory." (Colossians 3:3-4)

"Jesus said to him, "I am the way, and the truth, and the life; no one comes to the Father but through Me." (John 14:6)

"This is eternal life that they know me..." (John 17:3)

As we abide in Him and He abides in us, we are receiving His life rather than creating our own independent life. We draw our biological and spiritual life from Him, but this by no means eliminates our personalities or character development.
Our hearts have become Christ's dwelling place, and this truth grows more real in our awareness and experience as we lay hold of it by faith. (Ephesians 3:17)

We must move from focusing on being Christ-like to possessing Christ as life. He is the Christian life, it is not by works. It is lived by yielding to Him and stepping out in faith.

For Christ to be alive in us and be real in our everyday life, we must know Him at a heart level, take hold of who we are in Him, and allow Him to be released through us in our actions. This process is called "appropriating" Christ.

Practically speaking "appropriating" Christ starts with a growing intimacy that we have outlined in detail (seeking Him through prayer, the Word, worship, etc. Layered upon this is a belief and behavior of our secure identity of being in Christ which is characterized by the growth process of glorifying God and not ourselves, allowing God to meet our needs on His time table and in His ways, and knowing that we are significant because of what Christ has done and is doing rather than my self-effort to prove my spiritual growth.

"In Christ" we have a new identity and because of this Christ changes us. He has allowed your difficulties and your difficult times, He will see you through them.
"I can do all this through him who gives me strength. (Philippians 4:13)

"Your real, new self (which is Christ's and also yours, and yours just because it is His) will not come as long as you are looking for it. It will come when you are looking for Him. . . Give up yourself. And you will find your real self. Lose your life and you will save it. . . . Keep back nothing. Nothing that you have not given away will ever be really yours. Nothing in you that has not died will ever be raised from the dead. Look for yourself and you will find in the long run only hatred, loneliness, despair, rage, ruin, and decay. But look for Christ and you will find Him, and with Him everything else will be thrown in."
C. S. Lewis, Mere Christianity

The quality of your life now and your life in eternity is primarily determined by Hope.

Hope helps determine the quality of life today and in eternity by giving us a reason to live, by motivating us to invest and give wisely, to exercise faith in a right direction and to hold us fast in the storms of life. This is especially true when it comes to our stewarding the resources God has given us. Hope motivates us to grow spiritually and press through difficult times.

We are called to a lifestyle of generosity fixing our hope on God so that our destination and motivation will be glorifying the Lord, impacting God's Kingdom, and reaping an eternal reward that we will enjoy beginning now and lasting forever.

A.W. Tozer put it well in his devotional classic, The Knowledge of the Holy:
"The days of the years of our lives are few, and swifter than a weaver's shuttle. Life is a short and fevered rehearsal for a concert we cannot stay to give. Just when we appear to have attained some proficiency we are forced to lay our instruments down. There is simply not time enough to think, to become, to perform what the constitution of our natures indicates we are capable of. ...How completely satisfying to turn from our limitations to a God who has none? Eternal

years lie in His heart. For Him time does not pass, it remains; and those who are in Christ share with Him all the riches of limitless time and endless years."

Hope involves why we are here, what are our motivations, setting direction and priorities and handling difficulties all of which impact the quality of life. Hope is a motivator, does disappoint, and is what the world is looking for. In each of these ideas reflect on the verses that are behind it.

Hope is a Motivator

"And now these three remain: faith, hope and love. But the greatest of these is love". (1 Corinthians 13:13)

"Therefore, since we have such a hope, we are very bold." (2 Corinthians 3:12)

"But by faith we eagerly await through the Spirit the righteousness for which we hope." (Galatians 5:5)

"We continually remember before our God and Father your work produced by faith, your labor prompted by love, and your endurance inspired by hope in our Lord Jesus Christ." (1 Thessalonians 1:3)

"God did this so that, by two unchangeable things in which it is impossible for God to lie, we who have fled to take hold of the hope offered to us may be greatly encouraged."(Hebrews 6:18)

"Let us hold unswervingly to the hope we profess, for he who promised is faithful." (Hebrews 10:23)

"Be joyful in hope, patient in affliction, faithful in prayer." (Romans 12:12)

"I pray that the eyes of your heart may be enlightened, so that you will know what is the hope of His calling, what are the riches of the glory of His inheritance in

the saints, and what is the surpassing greatness of His power toward us who believe." (Ephesians 1:18, 19)

Hope does not disappoint

"And hope does not disappoint us, because God has poured out his love into our hearts by the Holy Spirit, whom he has given us." (Romans 5:5)

"But if we hope for what we do not yet have, we wait for it patiently." (Romans 8:25)

Hope is What the World is Looking For.

Let your hope be so attractive that you will be compelled to share Christ with others.
  "But in your hearts set apart Christ as Lord. Always be prepared to give an answer to everyone who asks you to give the reason for the hope that you have. But do this with gentleness and respect..." (1 Peter 3:15)

Hope helps one make a difference in your life

Hope is the difference between stepping out and never starting,
Hope is the difference between persevering and quitting,
Hope is the difference between sacrificing and holding on.
Hope is the difference between arriving and wandering aimlessly.
Hope is the difference between living and dying.

Making Hope Practical -
Gaining Order and Clarity in Regards to Our Finances.

Examine again 1 Timothy 6:17-19 at the beginning of this chapter. The connection of riches and hope is quite clear. Paul expressly says not to put our hope in the uncertainty of riches. Why is this? Riches do not satisfy, more is never enough, riches come and go, you can't take riches into eternity, and they can deceive us because riches give a temporary sense of lessening our needs and creating an independent spirit. We will see in the next several chapters that the way we handle our money is a spiritual discipline whereby we grow or decline.

Hope helps us to define things on the basis of their eternal value and thus we are motivated to give and be generous in regards to God's Kingdom purposes. Put into practice the heart of what James Dobson observes.

> "I have concluded that the accumulation of wealth, even if I could achieve it, is an insufficient reason for living. When I reach the end of my days, a moment or two from now I must look backward on something more meaningful than the pursuit of houses, land, machines, stocks and bonds. Nor is fame any lasting benefit. I will consider my earthly existence to have been wasted unless I can recall a loving family, a consistent investment in the lives of people and an earnest attempt to serve the God who made me. Nothing else makes much sense." Dr. James Dobson

Chapter 3 - Climbing Mountains and Living in the Valleys

"God allows us to experience the low points of life in order to teach us lessons that we could learn in no other way... We can ignore even pleasure. But pain insists upon being attended to. God whispers to us in our pleasures, speaks in our conscience, but shouts in our pains:
it is his megaphone to rouse a deaf world."
C.S. Lewis

"Climb mountains not so the world can see you,
but so you can see the world."
David McCullough, Jr.

Ken Boa discusses the road we will travel together.
"We are travelers on a quest, a voyage, an odyssey, a pilgrimage. If we are following Christ, we are headed for home, but there are stages along the way and lessons to be learned. This is why it is a mistake to view the spiritual life as a static condition or a state of being that can be attained by a combination of technique and information. To follow Christ is to move into territory that is unknown to us and to count on His purposeful guidance, His grace when we go off the path, and His presence when we feel alone. It is to learn to respond to God's providential care in deepening ways and to accept the pilgrim character of earthly existence with its uncertainties, setbacks, disappointments, surprises, and joys. It is to remember that we are in a pro-

cess of gradual conformity to the image of Christ so that we can love and serve others along the way."

We have set the stage with the reality of our days as the beginning point and hope as the future destination. This journey from here to there will require us to climb mountains yet make our home in the valleys in order to finish well. The chapter provides a map on the steps and process we will travel in order to walk with the Lord, be fruitful and have an impact.

We are going to examination a story told by jesus concerning the disciples and their fishing, with an eye to see the connection between surrender (motivation of the heart) and stewardship (strength for the hand).

"Now it happened that while the crowd was pressing around Him and listening to the word of God, He was standing by the lake of Gennesaret; and He saw two boats lying at the edge of the lake; but the fishermen had gotten out of them and were washing their nets. And He got into one of the boats, which was Simon's, and asked him to put out a little way from the land. And He sat down and began teaching the people from the boat. When He had finished speaking, He said to Simon, "Put out into the deep water and let down your nets for a catch." Simon answered and said, "Master, we worked hard all night and caught nothing, but I will do as You say and let down the nets." When they had done this, they enclosed a great quantity of fish, and their nets began to break; so they signaled to their partners in the other boat for them to come and help them. And they came and filled both of the boats, so that they began to sink. But when Simon Peter saw that, he fell down at Jesus' feet, saying, "Go away from me Lord, for I am a sinful man!" For amazement had seized him and all his companions because of the catch of fish which they had taken; and so also were James and John, sons of Zebedee, who were partners with Simon. And Jesus said to Simon, "Do not fear, from now on you will be catching men." When they had brought their boats to land, they left everything and followed

Him." (Luke 5:1-11)

In the story we see the disciples using their nets for fishing (stewardship of work) and we will observe different types of nets. We also will connect that to move from one type of net to the next takes a surrender of the heart. Stewardship relates to doing and surrender relates to being. We see the interplay of being and doing and how the being must be the fuel or motivation for change.

The Empty Net – No Fruit

The disciples go out fishing all night long, they are experienced, hard-working, and skilled in their in craft, yet they catch NOTHING! This is a picture of us trying to live the Christian life or manage our finances from our skills, capacity and know-how. It could be also know as the "flesh" which produces no fruit. Yes, your effort is hard-working, sincere, and well intentioned but the outcome is CHAOS. This can look like begin busy, exhausted, and ready to quit. Time is a critical factor at this stage. (the empty net is a picture of our stewardship of time (fishing night and day) The question is how do we use our time? Are our lives marked with selfish desires and pursuits of distraction and that never satisfy?

> **> Correction and Change**

The Lord allows this type empty net in our life until we come to that place of brokenness and surrender. This is a surrender of being ready to change or repent and listen to the Lord and His word for instructing in our lives. This is what the disciples do, they hear Jesus go out in the boat and teach. Notice the disciples must confess and acknowledge they can't catch fish in their own strength and then submit to Jesus' direction. We all must come to the place of admitting we can't and that Christ can, we must repent to change.

Engaged Net - Fruit

Jesus tells the disciples to go our fishing again and to do it according to His direction. They set out again to engage their nets in line with His will. This is a picture of living the life that Jesus desires for all of us – "to engage" and our engagement is satisfying, it is the first level of being fruitful. . We are available and useful in the Lord's hands. It is similar to Matthew 5:16 when Jesus tells us to let our light shine. The net is one of ORDER, Are we doing what we should be doing? Order can be largely characterized by our use of Talents. The engaged net represents our work and career. Are our talents aligned with the Lord's desires or are they used for selfish pursuits? Order begins to come when our daily activities and choices begin to align in a direction that is in submission to the Lord's will.

> Faithful Obedience

The disciples went fishing in spite of being reluctant, they obeyed and did it faithfully. This is an attitude of a surrendered heart. The instruction of Christ for my life does not at first make sense, my emotions say "no", and yet, we take a step of faith. This type of surrender is one of faithful obedience.

Overflowing Net – Much Fruit

From this place of obedience the nets begin to fill and then over-flow, so much that two boats are filled and begin to sink! When we faithfully obey we experience the blessing of obedience. The Lord brings us into His abundance – "the abundant life." We begin to take hold of or appropriate the fruit of the spirit – God working in our lives. On some level this is where we all want to be and stay. This net is one where we feel like we will be content and generous because we have an abundance. In reality this net represents MA-TURITY – too much has been given, much is required. Maturity is reflected in how we utilize the Treasures we have been entrusted with. These treasures are a picture of all of our possessions both physically and spiritually.

> Give Up Control and Ownership

There are two reactions in relation to the miracle. Peter recognizes he is in the presence of an awesome teacher, Jesus, and sees his woeful inadequacy, he sees his sinfulness. The rest of the disciples having seen the miracle of the overflowing net, they are struck with amazement or worship. Our lives should reflect these similar responses: my falling short and equally my worship of the Lord. Jesus encourages Peter and the rest of the disciples not to fear but leave their nets behind. In other words give up the control of their lives and the ownership of the fish. This level of surrender is much deeper than obedience, it is putting Christ on the throne.

Abandoned Net – Multiplying fruit

Jesus casts a vision for the rest of their lives – "from now on you will be catching men"! Their living will no longer be from fishing but from engaging and helping people – ministry. This life of ministry will produce fruit that multiplies. The disciples leave or abandon their nets. This net focuses on ETERNITY and God's Kingdom purposes. The resources we use in this stage is our Life. This net illustrates that our life is not our own, we follow the Lord.

>Following Christ

The action of the disciples is two-fold: they give up their fishing nets AND they follow Christ. They "go all in" on following Christ wherever that will take them.

In summary this story shows the intertwining of surrender (the motivation of the heart) and stewardship (strength for the hand). They go together, we can't have one with out the other. This is critical to having a flourishing life.

Climbing Mountains and Living in Valleys

We began our study by outlining a roadmap to "Flourishing in Troubling Times." Now let's look deeper at the subject. There are four "mountains" that we climb along the journey. Each of thee mountaintops has a practical and spiritual connection:

- Chaos: the storm & hope,
- Order: surrender/stewardship & managing finances,
- Maturity: contentment, generosity, and
- Eternity: living in the Kingdom.

There are also four major valleys we can live in and move through that will promote our growth and ability to flourish. These are:
- Correction and repentance,
- Pruning and abiding,
- Investing and sacrificing
- Persevering and following

We want to move quickly from one mountaintop to the next, yet life is not lived on top of mountains. Life is lived in the valleys. We can look at this two ways:
1. Valleys are the low points and difficulties both of which can be true and
2. Valleys are where one grows crops, finds streams of fresh water, and find refuge in the storms. If we are going to live in contentment we need to accept, be at peace, and even enjoy living in the valleys because is where we, too, grow and find the presence of the Lord. We will take a much deeper look at this issue in Chapter Three.

The parable of four nets is really a picture of the four mountains we must navigate in life to be true followers in God's Kingdom. These mountains are the four stages we journey. Mountaintops offer us the opportunity on gaining perspective, we can see where we are and where we need to go.

The challenge is that we can't live of the mountaintops as the weather is harsh and there is no or little water and vegetation

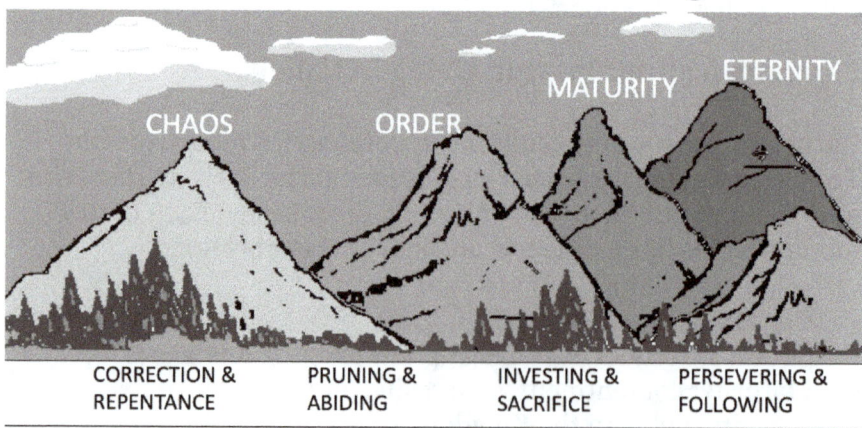

These mountaintops are hurdles or hallmarks of our actions that reflect spiritual growth and the practical living out of the Christian life. We see four types of nets: empty, engaged, overflowing, and abandoned with four levels of fruitfulness associated with them.

Mountain	Net	Stewardship of
CHAOS	Empty Net	Time
ORDER	Engaged Net	Talent
MATURITY	Overflowing Net	Treasure
ETERNITY	Abandoned Net	Career or Life

Life in the Valley

This illustrates successive and deeper levels of surrender required in order to move from level of intimate, heart relationship with the Lord to the next level. These are "the valleys" where we live and where we have our being - it is NOT easy. Valleys are good in that this is where you find water, food and plants grow and there is a level of protection from the storms of life. Fruit is borne in the valleys. Valleys also are known for a level of difficulties and pain. Life in the valley is a process that brings both good and hardship or surrender.

Those levels of surrender are:
• Correction and Repentance.
  We need to repent and change course by seeking the Lord and His word.

• Pruning and Abiding marked by "Faithful Obedience"
  We need to be trustworthy and put into practice Christ's teaching.

• Investing and Sacrifice
  We give our lives and possessions to help others. We live by surrendering our possessions on behalf of others.

• Persevering and Following
  Our lives are marked by Christ as our life, We surrender our whole life.
Being able to live in the valley is at the heart of being content.

When we make the best of where the Lord has placed us, we learn, improve, and move to a deeper level of spiritual intimacy and fruitfulness. This is at the heart of "flourishing", yet it takes time and faithfulness. Our end goal is to hear the Lord say to us— "well-done good and faithful servant".

At different stages of our life we bear varying levels of fruit. With each of these valleys, there is an underlying process the Lord is working in and through us. Let's examine John 15:1-5, 13, 16 to see the biblical picture.

"I am the true vine, and My Father is the vinedresser. Every branch in Me that does not bear fruit, He takes away; and every branch that bears fruit, He prunes it so that it may bear more fruit. You are already clean because of the word which I have spoken to you. Abide in Me, and I in you. As the branch cannot bear fruit of itself unless it abides in the vine, so neither can you unless you abide in Me. I am the vine, you are the branches; he who abides in Me and I in him, he bears much fruit, for apart from Me you can do nothing.

Greater love has no one than this, that one lay down his life for his friends. ...You did not choose Me but I chose you, and appointed you that you would go and bear fruit, and that your fruit would remain, so that whatever you ask of the Father in My name He may give to you."

Mountains:	**Levels of Fruit:**
CHAOS	No Fruit – vs1
ORDER	Fruit – vs2
MATURITY	More/Much Fruit - vs3-5
ETERNITY	Multiplying Fruit – vs 16

Valleys:	**Description**
CORRECTION	chastisement/repent
PRUNING/ABIDING	persevere/intimacy
INVESTING	ministry/love
FOLLOWING	well done faithful servant

Being able to live in the valley where we are and seek to grow spiritually so that we bear greater levels of fruit is at the heart of being content and being mature. We make the best of where we are, we learn, improve and move to a deeper level of spiritual intimacy and fruitfulness. This is at the heart of "flourishing", yet it takes time and faithfulness. Our end goal is to hear from the Lord – "well-done good and faithful servant".

Two Sides to Every Mountain

CHAOS

There are two types of people who journey and camp out on the mountain of Chaos.

They are the pre-Christian and the Baby Christian. These people have totally different hearts, yet outwardly are very similar in that they tend to be still focused on themselves and their needs. They make rather poor judgments in relationships and in the practical use of finances. Their lives are marked by many ups and downs emotionally, mentally, and spiritually. The have more than their fair share of challenges because they tend not to make great choices. There is little to no fruit in the spiritual lives.

Many people like to stay here because it is filled with fun, and entertainment that can outweigh the pain. It is only when the pain and its consequences become too unbearable that people consider making choices that lead to correction and a change of course. Correction and change is the only path to Order and one must climb the mountain of "order" before they can get to maturity.

See the chart on the next page.

Mountain – Stage	Two Sides of the Mountain	Heart Attitudes & Outcome	Fruit Level Characteristics
CHAOS – Baby	Pre-Christian – Selfish, self-centered, issues and problems abound	PAIN >> CHOICES	No Fruit
	Baby Christian - Committed to Christ, yet still infant in heart issues, need a lot of support, problems still exist. Need help.	We have pain and begin to see the need for and actually begin to make some wise choices. It is hard to live in Chaos ongoing.	Chaos is marked by SELF and all of the struggles and difficulties associated with it.
ORDER – Child	Surrender – The Lord is on the throne and we are daily dying to the flesh. First "Lifestyle Choice"	DISCIPLINE >> PEACE & FREEDOM	Fruit – some fruit is beginning to be seen.
	Stewardship – God is owner and we are managers of time, talent, treasure, truth, relationships, gospel	Choices become discipline and obedience. We exercise the spiritual disciplines: Prayer, Word, Silence, Solitude Exercise Wisdom	Order is a stage of choosing to walk by FAITH. We are confronted with the pull of the world and the things of the Lord.
MATURITY – Young Adult	Contentment – My life does not consist of possessions, power, or position. Marked by satisfaction and simplicity.	COMMITMENT >> SERVING

Faithful obedience and discipline leads to commitment and serving others. | Through pruning and abiding we bear More Fruit & Much Fruit |
| | Generosity – Become other centered and have great joy in giving away bountifully | Our Purpose becomes clarified | Maturity is marked by LOVE. We love the Lord and people and not the things of the world. |
| ETERNITY – Adult | Ministry – Begin to invest all resources to help others grow and reproduce. | PRESSING ON >> STAND

Life is marked by pressing on in spite of challenges, pressing into the Lord, and standing firm against the enemy. This world is home. | As we invest in people they begin to bear Fruit that multiplies. |
| | Kingdom – God is Glorified, people are changed, and we are fulfilled. | | We gain an eternal HOPE that is Kingdom and Christ focused. |

ORDER

The mountain of Order has two sides: surrender while going up and stewardship on the descent. Climbing the slope of surrender begins with a heart change that puts God in control of the process and results. People must make a Lordship decision of "kneeling before the Lord with palms up". This is a difficult ascent where each successive step can be harder and it is easy to slip backwards.

Climbers will need the support of other climbers, learn good climbing techniques, exercise discipline and utilize good equipment. There is a satisfaction as well as a sense of peace and freedom when this side of the mountain is mastered.

The downslope is that of stewardship – the practical giving up of my ownership and control of finances, times, talent, etc. This side of the journey requires an equal amount of discipline as it is also easy to slip and fall. Journeying on the mountain of Order takes FAITH, we can't see around the next corner, we simply must trust our guide. This part of the trip is rewarding and does yield an initial level of fruit.

On the mountain of Order people begin to grow and think for themselves. They are able to function on their own and grow spiritually. At his location, people love their peace and freedom, yet in many cases they are still focused on their own worlds – what they need, want, and desire. Peace and freedom can be a barrier to growth. People often like it is the goal and it is only a step along the way.

MATURITY

The mountain of Maturity reflects a journey that is more of the heart, relationships and reflects inner values rather than the activity associated with the mountain of order. The upslope of maturity is that of contentment, in other words being satisfied with what you have rather always pursing something more. Contentment is learned and marked by being satisfied with the Lord, His presence, and His gifts. Simplicity of life helps one live out this freedom. Contentment settles us on the inside so we can turn our attention, gifts and resources to others.

Generosity is a key mark of maturity, we are no longer consumed with filling our perceived needs but we focus on others. Generosity is not just for the affluent, it is a virtue for every individual because it is a generous gift given by the Lord to everyone. We see how generous God is with us, so we want to be generous with others. The mountain of "maturity" demonstrates LOVE – to others and to the Lord.

To move from "Order" to "Maturity" one goes through the valley of pruning and abiding. We are shaped through adversity to bear more fruit and it is in abiding with the Lord and entering into a deeper love relationship with the Lord we bear much fruit. Maturity with its characteristics of contentment and generosity is not the end goal of the Christian journey. It is a stop over, a place to enjoy, yet not the end.

ETERNITY

Our journey carries on to the mountain of eternity where the Lord is glorified, the world is impacted and we are fulfilled. The two sides to this mountain consist of ministry and Kingdom focus. Ministry is that place where we have already gone through the valley of investing and sacrificing our lives and our resources so now the focus is sharing the gospel and helping others walk with the Lord. It is a whole life investment. The backside of eternity is the Kingdom which is also our destination of HOPE. We are called to seek first the Kingdom of God and all these things will be added to you. The blessing of the mountain of "Eternity" is that now others who we have helped begin to bear fruit and start on their own journeys. We leave a legacy of multiplying fruit.

This mountain will not be without difficulty and struggle because the spiritual battle will intensify, you will have a mark on your back that the enemy wants to go after. We are called to stand against the rulers and forces of darkness while we continue to follow the Lord. Our reward will be the sound of "well done, good and faithful servant enter into the joy of your master."

Ten Observations

1. Climbing mountains and living in the valleys is a journey and process that is not linear. It is often two steps forward and one

step back. It has pitfalls and many ditches. Our lives should be marked by direction not perfection. Progress will come from the life and strength of Christ compelling us forward, not just our sheer effort, knowledge, and skills. It is a spiritual journey of growth in a real world of challenge. Our attitudes and actions towards finances are an excellent indicator of where we are on our journey.

2. This journey is not about speed or arriving first. We don't truly arrive until we breathe our last and see the face of the Lord. Thus the journey is more about faithfulness and perseverance than the pace. In fact we need to enjoy the moment and seize each day as if it is our last. Age does not mean progress, one can live as a one year old thirty times over.

3. Life on top of the mountains offers perspective, we see where we have come and where we are going. Life at the top can be cool and refreshing, yet offers little sustenance of water or food. The elements can be harsh and one is more exposed to them at this place.

4. Living in the valleys is marked by both good and difficulty. The good is that is where the water is, the plants and fruit is raised as well as other people live. We have protection from the storms of life. Yet the valleys also represent hard choices of surrender and giving up if we are to move forward.

5. Each mountain and each valley represent different stages and maturity levels of life as well as in the spiritual life. We are called to grow up and not live like children the rest of our days. We can move forward and backward from one stage to another due to unwise choices and the spiritual battle.

6. One can't make this journey alone, it takes support, care, love, nurture of one another to progress. We need community. There are different needs at each level that we need to be aware of.

7. The mountains and valleys don't define who we are, they do shape and allow us to grow into who we are from God's perspective.

8. Because we are complex people with many facets (relationships, finances, work, purpose, emotions, etc.) we can be at two different places at the same time. We can have maturity in relationships and chaos in finances. This will bring more challenges so each one needs a high level of reflection to observe where they are and how to move forward.

9. We will discover that we are never truly at home on this journey, we are made for a home in heaven, and we are aliens passing through this life. We are being prepared for heaven by how we walk in this world.

10. The attitudes of thankfulness, gratefulness, humility, being other centered, and spiritually thirsty will help us in every stage of this journey.

The Lord allows us to walk through the valley, in fact much of life is lived there, so we will see Him and grow in relationship with Him because we need Him. If we were always on top and doing well we would most likely forget the Lord and think too highly of ourselves. In the valley we will be a help to fellow strugglers and people on the journey of life with us. Finally in the valley we find we will need God's guidance in order to follow His purposes. The pursuit of God's purposes gives us a motivation far greater than the pursuit of this world's goods. They are trinkets and toys compared to the riches of Christ.

Many wander through life without a purpose, not knowing what they are supposed to be doing. Those people find themselves unhappy most of their lives because they don't enjoy what they do and because they lack a purpose. Or they know what they should do and are afraid of doing it because of all the what ifs and the false expectations that appear to be real.

Consider the words of A.W. Tozer,
    "In back of every wasted life is a bad philosophy, an erroneous conception of life's worth and purpose. The man who believes that he was born to get all he can will spend his life trying to get it. The man who believes he was created to enjoy fleshly pleasures will devote himself to pleasure seek-

ing; and if by a combination of favorable circumstance he manages to get a lot of fun out of life, his pleasures will all turn to ashes in his mouth at the last. He will find out too late that God made him too noble to be satisfied with those tawdry pleasures he had devoted his life to here under the sun."

The Woodcutter

Max Lucado tells the following parable of the Woodcutter. It is a good word that helps us realize that circumstances can give false readings and that ultimately God is in charge. Do not judge an event as good or bad without understanding the context and trusting the Lord for what He is doing that we don't see. Don't rush to conclusions or judgments.

"Once there was an old man who lived in a tiny village. Although poor, he was envied by all, For he owned a beautiful white horse. Even the king coveted his treasure. A horse like this had never been seen before—such was its splendor, its majesty, its strength.

People offered fabulous prices for the steed, but the old man always refused. "This horse is not a horse to me," he would tell them. "It is a person. How could you sell a person? He is a friend, not a possession. How could you sell a friend?" The man was poor and the temptation was great. But he never sold the horse.

One morning he found that the horse was not in the stable. All the village came to see him.

"You old fool," they scoffed, "we told you that someone would steal your horse. We warned you that you would be robbed. You are so poor. How could you ever hope to protect such a valuable animal? It would have been better to have sold him. You could have gotten whatever price you wanted. No amount would have been too high. Now the horse is gone, and you've been cursed with misfortune."

The old man responded, "Don't speak too quickly. Say only that the horse is not in the stable.
That is all we know; the rest is judgment. If I've been cursed or not, how can you know? How can you judge?"

The people contested, "Don't make us out to be fools! We may not be philosophers, but great philosophy is not needed. The simple fact that your horse is gone is a curse."

The old man spoke again. "All I know is that the stable is empty, and the horse is gone. The rest I don't know. Whether it be a curse or a blessing, I can't say. All we can see is a fragment. Who can say what will come next?"

The people of the village laughed. They thought that the man was crazy. They had always thought he was fool; if he wasn't, he would have sold the horse and lived off the money. But instead, he was a poor woodcutter, an old man still cutting firewood and dragging it out of the forest and selling it.

He lived hand to mouth in the misery of poverty. Now he had proven that he was, indeed, a fool. After fifteen days, the horse returned. He hadn't been stolen; he had run away into the forest.

Not only had he returned, he had brought a dozen wild horses with him. Once again the village people gathered around the woodcutter and spoke. "Old man, you were right and we were wrong. What we thought was a curse was a blessing. Please forgive us."

The man responded, "Once again, you go too far. Say only that the horse is back. State only that a dozen horses returned with him, but don't judge. How do you know if this is a blessing or not? You see only a fragment. Unless you know the whole story, how can you judge? You read only one page of a book. Can you judge the whole book? You read only one word of a phrase. Can you understand the entire phrase?

"Life is so vast, yet you judge all of life with one page or one word. All you have is a fragment!

Don't say that this is a blessing. No one knows. I am content with what I know. I am not perturbed by
what I don't."
"Maybe the old man is right," they said to one another. So they said little. But down deep, they knew he was wrong. They knew it was a blessing. Twelve wild horses had returned with one horse. With a little bit of work, the animals could be broken and trained and sold for much money.

The old man had a son, an only son. The young man began to break the wild horses. After a few days, he fell from one of the horses and broke both legs. Once again the villagers gathered around the old man and cast their judgments.

"You were right," they said. "You proved you were right. The dozen horses were not a blessing.

They were a curse. Your only son has broken his legs, and now in your old age you have no one to help you. Now you are poorer than ever."

The old man spoke again. "You people are obsessed with judging. Don't go so far. Say only that my son broke his legs. Who knows if it is a blessing or a curse? No one knows. We only have a fragment. Life comes in fragments."

It so happened that a few weeks later the country engaged in war against a neighboring country. All the young men of the village were required to join the army. Only the son of the old man was excluded, because he was injured. Once again the people gathered around the old man, crying and screaming because their sons had been taken. There was little chance that they would return. The enemy was strong, and the war would be a losing struggle. They would never see their sons again.

"You were right, old man," they wept. "God knows you were right. This proves it. Yours son's accident was a blessing. His legs may be broken, but at least he is with you. Our sons are gone forever."

The old man spoke again. "It is impossible to talk with you. You always draw conclusions. No one knows. Say only this: Your sons had to go to war, and mine did not. No one knows if it is a blessing or a curse. No one is wise enough to know. Only God knows."

Conclusion: The old man was right. We only have a fragment. Life's mishaps and horrors are only a page out of a grand book. We must be slow about drawing conclusions. We must reserve judgment on life's storms until we know the whole story.

I don't know where the woodcutter learned his patience. Perhaps from another woodcutter in Galilee. For it was the Carpenter who said it best:
> "Do not worry about tomorrow, for tomorrow will worry about itself." (Matthew 6:33-34)

He should know. He is the author of our story. And he has already written the final chapter.

Applications

Keep your eyes open, learn where you are and be a student of how to move forward.

Assess and reflect where you are.

Seek wisdom and guidance from fellow travelers. You can't go alone.

Embrace the journey, enjoy each day and each relationship.

Accept the pains and difficulties as stepping stones and a means of growing.

Be willing to take risks of faith, make deposits of life, and keep your hope alive.

Next Steps of Our Journey

This chapter is a map for mountains and valleys we will face. The rest of the book will break down the mountains and guide through the valleys to prepare us to see Jesus.

ORDER
Chapter 4: Surrendering that Leads to Stewardship
Chapter 5: Making Lifestyles Choices That Order Your Finances

MATURITY
Chapter 6: Learning Contentment
Chapter 7: Exercising Generosity

ETERNITY
Chapter 8: Investing In Eternity
Conclusion: Answering God's Call

Chapter 4 - Surrendering Leads to Stewardship

"Childlike surrender and trust, I believe, is the defining spirit of authentic discipleship."
Brennan Manning

"We can only learn to know ourselves and do what we can - namely, surrender our will
and fulfill God's will in us."
Saint Teresa of Avila

"Surrendering means giving something over to God then replacing it with something from Him."
Kevin Martineau

Our first step in the journey is to move one from the mountain of CHAOS to the mountain of ORDER. This takes a process of surrender and stewardship. Surrender is the willful giving up of the control and results of our lives and allowing the Lord to rule and reign. Stewardship is measured by our faithfulness and is rewarded with being given greater opportunity and responsibility. If we are faithful, we will be given the true riches – eternal riches. We also note that we can only pursue and serve one master either the Lord or worldly resources. The choice is ours. The spiritual aspect of this is surrender and the practical side is how we steward our finances. This begins to put us on the road to order and bearing fruit.

We will begin with Jesus' story of the unrighteous steward.

"Now He was also saying to the disciples, "There was a rich man who had a manager, and this manager was reported to him as squandering his possessions. And he called him and said to him, 'What is this I hear about you? Give an accounting of your management, for you can no longer be manager.' The manager said to himself, 'What shall I do, since my master is taking the management away from me? I am not strong enough to dig; I am ashamed to beg. I know what I shall do, so that when I am removed from the management people will welcome me into their homes.' And he summoned each one of his master's debtors, and he began saying to the first, 'How much do you owe my master?' And he said, 'A hundred measures of oil.' And he said to him, 'Take your bill, and sit down quickly and write fifty.' Then he said to another, 'And how much do you owe?' And he said, 'A hundred measures of wheat.' He *said to him, 'Take your bill, and write eighty.' And his master praised the unrighteous manager because he had acted shrewdly; for the sons of this age are more shrewd in relation to their own kind than the sons of light. And I say to you, make friends for yourselves by means of the wealth of unrighteousness, so that when it fails, they will receive you into the eternal dwellings.

"He who is faithful in a very little thing is faithful also in much; and he who is unrighteous in a very little thing is unrighteous also in much. Therefore if you have not been faithful in the use of unrighteous wealth, who will entrust the true riches to you? And if you have not been faithful in the use of that which is another's, who will give you that which is your own? No servant can serve two masters; for either he will hate the one and love the other, or else he will be devoted to one and despise the other. You cannot serve God and wealth." (Luke 16:1-13)

What are the lessons from this parable?
Several are key: stewardship or our handling of resources is mea-

sured and reflected by faithfulness.
The Lord gives use resources to test and see just how faithful are we – a little or much? Our faithfulness will have a reward.

The next lesson is 'who is our master?' – the Lord or our wealth? Jesus states that we will have only one master. This is also found in Matthew 6:24,

> *"No one can serve two masters. Either you will hate the one and love the other, or you will be devoted to the one and despise the other. You cannot serve both God and money."*

The question becomes which is your master? Who or what owns us – God or money? Interestingly the word money here actually is the word 'mammon' which is an evil force associated with money but far more powerful. This mammon can grip us and control our thoughts and attitudes.

The choice is ours – to whom do we submit? or surrender the heart. We will choose either the Lord or money. The nature of that surrender is all encompassing, we don't half surrender – it is all or nothing.

This surrender involves all of our choices because when we surrender we give up control and determining the result today and ongoing.

This surrender of the heart can be further examined by six lifestyle choices that each of us must make if we are to follow the Lord with a whole heart

Six Lifestyle Choices

Choices are reflective of our character and the nature of a Godly character in our lives is to have an obedient heart – choosing to follow the Lord above all else. It is a desire to BE pleasing to God and to DO the will of God in all things.
This requires being broken rather than being proud.

The chart below gives us insight into the heart condition of these two kinds of people.
These choices begin with relinquishing our pride and embracing our brokenness.

NATURE	CHOICE	VERSE	QUESTION
Personal	Decease or Increase	John 3:30	Who is first in my life?
Strength	Weak or Strong	2 Corinthians 12:9-11	Can we overcome any obstacle?
Power	Received or Achieved	John 15:5	Who is the source of power?
Relation-ships	Give or Take	Acts 20:35	Who do I help?
Material	Possess or Let Go	Matthew 6:24	Who or what is the master?
Process	Entitled or Faithful	Luke 16:12	How are you doing?

John 12:24 provides us with a promise that ties being fruitful and flourishing to being broken and surrendered,

"Truly, truly, I say to you, unless a grain of wheat falls into the earth and dies, it remains alone; but if it dies, it bears much fruit."

Surrender and choosing to put the Lord in control is much easier said than done and it is a daily choice which is seen in Luke 9:23,

"And He was saying to them all, "If anyone wishes to come after Me, he must deny himself, and take up his cross daily and follow Me."

We who know Christ are called to surrender our will unconditionally to the Lord. God, however, has given us the freedom to choose whether to surrender.

Unlike the vanquished in war, our decision to surrender is motivated by the Lord's unconditional love for us not that we are a defeated foe. Our surrender is an act of worship.

"Therefore, I urge you, brothers, in view of God's mercy, to offer your bodies as living and sacrifices, holy and pleasing to God—this is your spiritual act of worship" (Romans 12:1)

Charles Spurgeon said,

"A primary qualification for serving God with any degree of success and for doing His work well and triumphantly is a sense of our own weakness. When the Lord's warrior marches forth to battle, strong in his own might or when he boasts, "I know I will be victorious, for my own mighty arm and conquering sword will give me the victory," defeat is not far away. God will not go forward with the person who marches ahead in his own strength. He who counted on victory in this fashion has counted wrongly, for "Not by might nor by power, but by my Spirit,' says the Lord Almighty" (Zech 4:6). Those who enter the battle boasting of their own process will return with their victory banners dragging through the dust and their armor stained with disgrace.

God will empty you of yourself before He will put His resources in you, cleaning out your granary before filling it with the finest of his wheat. The river of the Lord is full of water, but not one drop of it flows from earthly springs. He will never allow any strength to be used in His battles except that which He Himself imparts. eliever, are you mourning your own weakness? Take courage, for you must have an awareness of your own weakness before the Lord will give you victory. Your emptiness is the necessary preparation for being filled, and being cast down is simply preparing you to be lifted up.

Many Facets of Surrender

When we use the term surrender it can have many synonyms, descriptions and postures biblically: broken, repent, give up, or conformed. In this various postures that reveal principles that lead to processes at work resulting in God producing His outcomes.

Review the chart on the next page, in which you could symbolically transfer all your possessions back to God, and reflect on the bigger picture of surrender and how God uses this act in our individual lives as well as to advance His Kingdom purposes.

DEED OF OWNERSHIP

This Deed of Ownership is made the _____ day of _____

From: _____

To: The Lord

On this day I/we acknowledge God's ownership and my/our stewardship responsibility of the following:

ITEMS:

Stewards of the above listed
possessions:

(Optional) witnesses who hold
me/us accountable in the
recognition of the Lord's ownership:

_____

_____

_____

_____

Jesus Christ Modeled Surrender

In the life of Christ, we see that He completely humbled and submitted himself to His Heavenly Father, so that God was free to work powerfully through Him. Here are some examples of Christ humbling Himself to His Father. Note how Jesus used the words nothing referring to Himself.

"The Son can do nothing of Himself." (John 5:19)

"I [Jesus] can do nothing of My own initiative, as I hear, I judge; and My judgment is just; because I do not seek My own will but the will of Him who sent Me." (John 5:30)

Are You Willing To Surrender?

Jesus was willing to surrender to God, and He tells us in Luke 9:23, "If anyone wishes to come after Me, he must deny Himself, and take up his cross daily and follow Me."

It requires nothing less than a transformation of our hearts to submit to Christ as Lord, as our Life, and as the Leader. Because of our own pride and the world's perspective of leadership that is so deeply ingrained in most of us, it can require years and often difficult circumstances to completely humble ourselves and embrace God's way of life.

In the 1600s, Francois Fenelon, wrote a letter to his friends in prison that capture this understanding:

"And the very proof that God loves you is that He does not spare you, but lays upon you the cross of Jesus Christ. Whatever spiritual knowledge or feelings we may have, they are all a delusion if they do not lead us to the real and constant practice of dying to self. And it is true that we do not die without suffering. Nor is it possible to be considered truly dead while there is any part of us which is yet alive.

"This spiritual death (which is really a blessing in disguise) is undeniably painful. It cuts "swift and deep into our innermost thoughts and desires with all their parts, exposing us for what we really are." The great Physician, who sees in us what we cannot see, knows exactly where to place the knife. He cuts away that which we are most reluctant to give up. And how it hurts! But we must remember that pain is only felt where there is life, and where there is life is just the place where death is needed."

Letting Go of Control and Results

One of the great enemies of spiritual growth and flourishing is the craving to control our environment and the desire to determine the results of our endeavors. We cannot be responsive to God's purposes until we abandon our strategies to control and acknowledge His exclusive ownership of our lives. Many of us have a natural inclination to be manipulators, grabbers, owners, and controllers. The more we seek to rule our world, the more we will resist the rule of Christ; those who grasp are afraid of being grasped by God. But until we relinquish ownership of our lives, we will not experience the relief of surrender to God's good purposes.

Dr. Ken Boa reinforces this thought,
"Our resistance to God's rule even extends to our prayerful attempts to persuade the Lord to bless our plans and to meet our needs in the ways we deem best. Instead of seeking God's will in prayer, we hope to induce Him to accomplish our will. Thus, even in our prayers, we can adopt the mentality of a consumer rather than a servant. We have little control over opportunities we encounter and the outcomes of our efforts, but we can be obedient to the process."

God is the Owner

In order to put the heart condition of surrender into practice we need to look at our finances and how we handle money. Our use of money is an outward indication of our spiritual condition and walk with the Lord.

So, who owns your money and finances? The world tells us we do and our flesh craves for this to be so. Yet biblically the case is just the opposite. Look at who is the owner in 1 Chronicles 29:11-12,

"Yours, O Lord, is the greatness, the power, the glory, the victory, and the majesty. Everything in the heavens and on earth is yours, O Lord, and this is your kingdom. We adore you as the one who is over all things. Wealth and honor come from you alone, for you rule over everything. Power and might are in your hand, and at your discretion people are made great and given strength."

And what does God own?

"The earth is the Lord's, and all it contains, the world, and those who dwell in it." (Psalms 24:1)

Many others verses indicate that God owns all of the wealth, the gold, silver, and even the cattle on a thousand hills.

Clearly God is the owner and thus we assume the role of steward or manager. This is where the rubber meets the road, we must engage in the practical application of giving up the ownership of our wealth, finances, and life to pursue a radical lifestyle of serving the Lord with large consequences and implications.

Our Role as Faithful Steward Begins with Surrender

The key verse that describes our role in life and in our finances is 1 Corinthians 4:2,

"moreover, it is required of stewards that one be found trustworthy."

A manager is defined as "a person responsible for and in charge of administering all or part of a company or similar organization that is not their own." Managers have a full level of responsibility and must be trustworthy and skilled to function well. This applies in particular to how we handle our finances. The Lord calls us to be first faithful – someone in whom the Lord can trust with using the money and resources wise and well. Not only does the Lord count on us to be a good manager, our families need us to be faithful stewards also or there will be more chaos in the relationships around us. .

Faithfulness is a reflection of our character and is a quality that can be learned and improved. We grow in faithfulness by doing little things well and then we can be entrusted with more. Read Luke 16:10-13,

> *"He who is faithful in a very little thing is faithful also in much; and he who is unrighteous in a very little thing is unrighteous also in much. Therefore if you have not been faithful in the use of unrighteous wealth, who will entrust the true riches to you? And if you have not been faithful in the use of that which is another's, who will give you that which is your own?"*

The New Testament word for stewardship is oikonomia, from which we derive the word economy. This word means "management of a household," and it refers to the responsibility that is entrusted to a manager. A steward acts as an administrator of the affairs and possessions of another. Stewards are fully accountable to their masters and may act justly as did Joseph who became Potiphar's steward (Genesis 39:4-6), or unjustly as in Christ's parable of the steward who squandered his master's possessions (Luke 16:1-13). As Christians, we have been entrusted with a stewardship; the things we call our own are not really ours, but God's. We have no possessions, and we do not even own ourselves:

> *"Or do you not know that your body is a temple of the Holy Spirit who is in you, whom you have from God, and that you are not your own? For you have been bought with a price: therefore glorify God in your body" (1 Corinthians 6:19-20; cf. 3:23).*

Since we belong to Christ, we no longer have the right to self-determination.

Faithfulness has a focus of pleasing the Lord and not working or doing something for selfish gain. Note the quote by Charles Stanley.

It takes a secure and humble leader to be able to serve others and help them succeed.

As long as we insist on writing our own stories, He cannot write His living will onto our hearts.
As long as we insist on forging our own paths, He cannot lead us into His paths of righteousness.
As long as we insist on governing our own lives, He cannot be our Sovereign King and Lord.
As long as we insist on living life according to our own desires, He cannot impart His desires or guide us into His wholeness, fruitfulness, and blessings.
As long as we feel that we are in control of our fate, we cannot experience fully the destiny he has for us. We are His workmanship. When we act otherwise, we are breaching our trust relationship with God and are refusing to submit our lives fully to Him.

Whole Life Stewardship

We are called to be managers of not only our the finances but of a number of other resources that the Lord has graciously given to us. This is called "whole life stewardship". There are 7 areas where the Lord gives us resources and gifts to be used by Him in us and on His behalf: Time, Talent, Treasure, Truth, Relationships, Gospel, and Grace.

Take time for example; our time on earth is not controlled by us whether short or long, what we do control is how we use it either for selfish gain or for extending God's kingdom purposes. We can learn time management to better use our time because our time on earth is limited and once spent can never be regained.

The Lord gives us talents and gifts such as the innate ability to work with people or numbers, etc. Again we can grow and learn in these areas to order to improve, yet we are all uniquely different but wonderfully made and gifted. The Lord also fashions us with a distinct personality that is uniquely ours. The question is how are we investing our gifts? We need to realize and embrace the fact that all of life is gift and grace, we don't deserve and cannot earn it.

We are called to manage it wise and well

Our Attitude - Thankfulness

We have concluded we are not in control of the results and circumstances of our lives, yet we do exercise a level of control of how we play our cards.. Do we exercise faithfulness? Can God and others count on our being trustworthy. The second element is our attitude, are we thankful in all situations whether good or bad. Note the teaching in 1 Thessalonians 5:18. "in everything give thanks; for this is God's will for you in Christ Jesus." Thankfulness is a major hallmark for a Christian and is one of the most practical, simple of the disciplines.

> *"you will be enriched in everything for all liberality, which through us is producing thanksgiving to God." (2 Corinthians 9:11)*

> *"Be anxious for nothing, but in everything by prayer and supplication with thanksgiving let your requests be made known to God." (Philippians 4:6)*

> *"Devote yourselves to prayer, keeping alert in it with an attitude of thanksgiving;" (Colossians 4:2)*

> *"But thanks be to God, who always leads us in triumph in Christ, and manifests through us the sweet aroma of the knowledge of Him in every place." (2 Corinthians 2:14)*

> *"For all things are for your sakes, so that the grace which is spreading to more and more people may cause the giving of thanks to abound to the glory of God." (2 Corinthians 4:15)*

The following quotation is by Ravi Zacharias.

"I think of the powerful testimony of a woman named Annie Johnston Flint. She was one who lived most of her life in pain. Orphaned early in life, her body was embarrassed by incontinence, weakened by cancer, and twisted and deformed by rheumatoid arthritis. She was incapacitated for so long that according to one eyewitness she needed seven or eight pillows around her body just to cushion the raw sores she suffered from being bedridden. Yet her autobiography is rightly called The Making of the Beautiful. Almost like a minstrel from heaven she penned words that touch the heart in its despairing moments. One of her best-known poems, put to music, reads:

'He giveth more grace when the burdens grow greater,
He sendeth more strength when the labors increase;
Too added affliction, He addeth His mercy,
To multiplied trials His multiplied peace.

When we have exhausted our store of endurance,
When our strength has failed e're the day is half done,
When we reach the end of our hoarded resources
Our Father's full giving has only begun.

His love has no limits, His grace has no measure,
His power has no boundary known unto men;
For out of His infinite riches in Jesus
He giveth, and giveth, and giveth again!'"

Seeing only the negative aspects of any situation can cause you to miss opportunities, neglect problems that need to be solved, and fail to take action that would otherwise improve your relationships and quality of life. In fact, studies show that pessimists are more likely to develop chronic illnesses later on in life than optimists.

Optimists look for the light at the end of the tunnel. If you've always had a pessimistic worldview, it can be difficult to shift your focus, but it is possible to start seeing the glass as half full, not half empty. In fact you may come to realize that glasses are generally full - it's just that gravity attracts the more dense liquid material towards the bottom.

Summary

To live a life that flourishes we recognize where we are (reality and where we want to go (hope). Then we begin with an examination of our heart toward the Lord and in practical terms of how we handle money. We conclude that we must live a surrendered life – one that puts and keeps God on the throne and us serving Him. From here we recognize that the Lord is the owner of all, He controls every circumstance and He promises to meet our every need. Our part is to be a faithful steward or manager. We are to be stewards of our whole life - Time, Talent, Treasure, Truth, Relationships, Gospel, and Grace. From stewardship we are to exercise thankfulness in all things.

The challenge we will face is that you will have push back on this from the world and even well meaning Christians. Stewardship is not easy. Society says that you earned your money and now you can spend it anyway you choose and you will be happy. The Word tells us to be faithful stewards. Note the follow thoughts from George Barna.

George Barna noted,

"Almost every great biblical hero was broken by God through multiple life crises or harsh circumstances designed for that purpose. There is no getting around the reality: even the best of us needs to be broken, fully and completely detached from our dalliance with sin, self, and society.

If you examine the individuals involved in all these instances, you'll see that God does not force us to accept brokenness. He always allows us to choose. But if you are wise, you will discover that you either allow God to use circumstances to wake you and break you, or you may count on continuing to fight Him and suffer.

Most people never realize that brokenness is actually a gift from God that demonstrates His awesome and unyielding love. We typically examine the circumstances designed to guide us from a casual acquaintance to an intense and intimate lover of God and foolishly conclude that they are harmful to our well-being. In reality, they are God's means of bringing us to our knees before Him, in full-on repentance, enabling us to see the truth of who we are, who He is, how we treat Him, and how compassionate He is.

In our culture-aided confusion we focus on the deprivation, sacrifice, pain, suffering, hardship, and persecution that God injects into our experience. We mistakenly assume that once we believe nice things about God and invest a few personal resources in the development of our faith, the appropriate response by our Father should be affirmation, comfort, pleasure, rewards, and happiness."

Practical Application

A deed is used to transfer ownership of possession from one person to another. If you are convicted that you should transfer everything you own back to God, the rightful owner, here is your opportunity to do so. Take note of the deed on the next page, fill it in and sign in the presence of other witnesses of your application of the stewardship principle.

Chapter 5 - Ordering Your Finances

"We buy stuff we don't need with money we don't have to impress people we don't like."
George Carlin

"Money never made a man happy yet, nor will it. The more a man has, the more he wants.
Instead of filling a vacuum, it makes one."
Benjamin Franklin

Connecting the Spiritual with the Practical

Dr. Larry Burkett, a teacher on helping the common person have victory in their finances, said this,
"The way we handle money is an outward indicator of an inward spiritual condition."
The truth in this statement is astounding and most people never connect the dots. We tend to err on one side of the coin or the other, either we are focused on the Lord and His mission while lacking the discipline to handle our money or we our very detailed about money with little or no connection to the spiritual life. We need both. We have laid a strong spiritual foundation, now we will directly the spiritual to how we think and handle our resources.

Jesus Teaches on Being Prepared

In the following passage Jesus is instructing the disciples specifically about being prepared, being on alert, and being a faithful steward. We are to manage our resources well or there will be severe consequences in this life and in the life to come. If we are faithful we will be invited to ask for more!

"Be dressed in readiness, and keep your lamps lit. Be like men who are waiting for their master when he returns from the wedding feast, so that they may immediately open the door to him when he comes and knocks. Blessed are those slaves whom the master will find on the alert when he comes; truly I say to you, that he will gird himself to serve, and have them recline at the table, and will come up and wait on them. Whether he comes in the second watch, or even in the third, and finds them so, blessed are those slaves. "But be sure of this, that if the head of the house had known at what hour the thief was coming, he would not have allowed his house to be broken into. You too, be ready; for the Son of Man is coming at an hour that you do not expect."

Peter said, "Lord, are You addressing this parable to us, or to everyone else as well?" And the Lord said, "Who then is the faithful and sensible steward, whom his master will put in charge of his servants, to give them their rations at the proper time? Blessed is that slave whom his master finds so doing when he comes. Truly I say to you that he will put him in charge of all his possessions.

But if that slave says in his heart, 'My master will be a long time in coming,' and begins to beat the slaves, both men and women, and to eat and drink and get drunk; the master of that slave will come on a day when he does not expect him and at an hour he does not know, and will cut him in pieces, and assign him a place with the unbelievers. And that slave who knew his master's will and did not get ready or act in accord with his will, will receive many lashes, but the one who did not know it, and committed deeds worthy of a flogging, will receive but few. From everyone who has been given much, much will be required; and to whom they entrusted much, of him they will ask all the more." (Luke 12:35-48)

In order for us to "Flourish" we must acknowledge God's ownership and our role as steward. Then we need to be practical and diligent to bring order to our finances. We must move out of chaos and bondage. We will briefly examine four areas of financial discipline: debt, spending, saving and giving.

Compass has a tool: "Navigating your Finances God's Way: which is a comprehensive bible study that will help you.

Debt

What is the Lord's heart on debt? Read Romans 13:8 from several different translations:

"Owe no man anything" (KJV).
"Let no debt remain outstanding" (NIV).
"Pay all your debts" (TLB).
"Owe nothing to anyone" (NASB).
"Keep out of debt and owe no man anything" (Amplified).

The Lord does not want us in debt because we will be in slavery or bondage to the one we owe money. I Corinthians 7:23 says,

"You were bought with a price; do not become slaves of men."

Here's why the Lord wants you debt-free.

1. DEBT IS A FORM OF BONDAGE

"Just as the rich rule the poor, so the borrower is servant to the lender." (Proverbs 22:7)

When we're in debt, we're a servant to the lender. And the deeper we are in debt, the more like servants we become. We don't have the freedom to decide where to spend our income, because it's already obligated to meet our debt payments.

2. DEBT WAS CONSIDERED A CURSE.

"If you diligently obey the Lord your God, being careful to do all His commandments which I command you today, the Lord your God will set you high above all the nations of the earth. All these blessings will come upon you.... You shall lend to many nations, but you

shall not borrow" (Deuteronomy 28:1-2, 12)
In the Old Testament, being out of debt was one of the promised rewards for obedience.

3. DEBT PRESUMES UPON TOMORROW.

"You who say, 'Today or tomorrow, we shall go to such and such a city, and spend a year there and engage in business and make a profit.' Yet you do not know what your life will be like tomorrow.... Instead, you ought to say, 'If the Lord wills, we shall live and also do this or that'" (James 4:13-15)

When we get into debt, we're assuming that we will earn enough in the future to repay it. But can we really assume such a thing? We plan for our jobs to continue or our investments to be profitable. The Bible strongly cautions us against such presumption. "

4. DEBT SATIFIES A SHORT DESIRE, NOT NECESSARILY A NEED

Our desire to get things now and then going in debt may circumvent God to work and provide. We often go into debt because we want something now. We did not get into debt overnight and we won' get out of debt overnight. The following is a checklist or guide of how to get out of debt. Start by praying – let God in on your issues both to guide and direct but also to encourage us.

The Process to Being Debt-free

Here is a simple roadmap to getting out of debt.
1. Trust God to help you
2. Establish a Written Budget
3. List Your Assets - List everything God has entrusted you to manage.
4. List Your Liabilities - You now have an accurate picture of your finances.
5. Snowball Your Debt
   Stop investing (unless fpr your retirement fund), only pay minimum debt payments.
   Start with credit cards – lowest balance first
   Apply that payment to the next credit card / debt.
   Repeat until all debt is eliminated.

6. Earn Additional Income - There are only two ways to get out of debt – earn more & spend less.
7. Accumulate No new Debt
8. Be Content With What You Have
   The more you watch TV, the more you spend.
   The more you look at catalogs, the more you spend.
   The more you shop, the more you spend.
9. Consider a Radical Change in your Lifestyle
10. Do Not Give Up!

Some Additional Ideas:

Earn additional income. Many people hold jobs that simply don't pay enough to allow them to pay off their debts quickly enough.

Spend less by becoming content with what you have. Advertisers use powerful methods to get us to buy. Frequently the message is intended to foster discontentment with what we have. There is an interesting passage in 1 Timothy 6:5-6. When we are content with what we have and wait to buy until we can do it using cash—that is great gain.

Snowball your way out of debt. And here's how. In addition to making the minimum payments on all your credit cards, focus on paying off the smallest-balance-card first. You'll be encouraged to see its balance go down, down, and finally disappear! After the first credit card is paid off, apply its payment toward the next-smallest one. After the second card is paid off, apply what you were paying on the first and second toward the third-smallest. That's the snowball in action!

When you're on a roll like this, it starts getting exciting. Those "impossible" balances that have worried you and robbed you of your peace will begin diminishing before your very eyes. So...where do you start? Prioritize your debts. And every time you pay one of those cards off, use it as an occasion to celebrate and thank the Lord!

Spending (Establishing a Budget)

You need to get a hold of how much you are spending. Record

everything. Choose to use either the envelop method or a very clear yet simple ledger. You must have an accurate understanding of what you are spending and then begin to make a plan of what are the priorities and what can you cut back. A budget helps takes away emotional tug that happens when you see something you want, yet don't know if your have the means of paying for it. You ask yourself – "Is it in the budget?" You then let the budget make the decision not your feelings.

Saving

The Bible encourages us to save. Savings is all about not spending today (generally a want) so that you'll have something to spend in the future (a need). Most people are poor savers because they don't see the value in practicing self-denial or don't want to exercise discipline. Our culture screams that we "deserve" to get what we want, when we want it! The most effective way to save is to make it automatic.

> *"Ah, my Lord GOD! You made the heavens and the earth with your great power and your outstretched arm; nothing is too difficult for you." (Jeremiah 32:17)*

> *"The wise man saves for the future, but the foolish man spends whatever he gets" (Proverbs 21:20, TLB)*

> God commends the ant for saving. *"Four things on earth are small, yet they are extremely wise: ants are creatures of little strength, yet they store up their food in the summer" (Proverbs 30:24-25)*

Lastly, in Genesis 41:29-30, we rad of how Joseph saved a fifth of all that came in during "seven years of great abundance in order to survive during "seven years of famine"

Giving

The Lord calls us to give as a matter of spiritual discipline and growth. In giving we experience the Lord working through us and we participate in God's Kingdom work. Gifts obviously benefit the recipient such as the church continues its ministry, the hungry are fed, the naked are clothed, and missionaries are sent. In God's economy, gifts given with the proper attitude benefit the giver more than the receiver. Giving is greatly encouraged by Jesus Christ Himself in Acts 20:35,

"It is more blessed to give than receive."

When we examine scripture, we find that the giver benefits in four significant areas.

1. An Increase in Intimacy. Above all else, giving directs our hearts to Christ. This is why it's necessary to give each gift to the person of Jesus Christ: it draws our hearts to Him. (Matthew 6:21)

2. An Increase in Character. Our heavenly Father wants us—His children—to be conformed to the image of His Son. The character of Christ is that of an unselfish giver. Unfortunately, humans are selfish by nature. One essential way we become conformed to Christ is by regular giving. Someone once said, "Giving is not God's way of raising money; it is God's way of raising people into the likeness of His Son."

3. An Increase in Heaven. The Lord tells us that heaven has its own "First National Bank," where we can invest for eternity.
"But store up for yourselves treasures in heaven, where neither moth nor rust destroys, and where thieves do not break in or steal; for where your treasure is, there your heart will be also." (Matthew 6:20-21)

4. An Increase on Earth. Many people have a hard time believing that giving results in material blessings flowing back to the giver. Time and again, however, we encounter that very truth in the pages of Scripture.
"Give, and it will be given to you. They will pour into your lap a good measure—pressed down, shaken together, and running over. For by your standard of measure it will be measured to you in return." (Luke 6:38)

Practical Application

Consider a radical change in lifestyle. A growing number of people have lowered their standard of living significantly to get out of debt more quickly. Some have downsized their homes, rented apartments, or moved in with family members. Sell what you're not using. Evaluate your possessions to determine whether you should sell any of them to help you get out of debt more quickly. What about the clothes you no longer wear? Those fishing rods gathering dust? Is there anything you can sell to help you get out of debt?

The Circle of Spending

"I just don't know where it all goes! The month is not finished and we're short already." This seems to be a common phenomenon, affecting people with all sizes of income. No matter much money we earn, there always seems to be more month than money! It is a well-known saying that "money talks", but all mine seems to say is 'Goodbye'!

It seems to have been a problem in the Old Testament times. The prophet Haggai passed on Gods words. "Now, therefore, thus says the Lord of hosts: Consider your ways. You have sown much and harvested little. You eat, but you never have enough; you drink, but you never have your fill. You clothe yourselves, but no one is warm. And he who earns wages does so to put them into a bag with holes." (Haggai 1:5,6)

God is asking us to consider our ways. He is inviting us to adjust our lives to his ways. Haggai's picture of bags with holes is a powerful image. God does not want us to just patch up our bags and wait for things to get back to normal. Instead, we must find a new way of living as faithful stewards of all that God has given to us. Don't patch the bags; get new bags!

The secret to financial success is very easy. Spend less than you earn over a long period of time and you will be financially successful. To do this we need to setup a spending plan, together with God who is the owner of our money, to plan our finances so that each month we are spending less than is coming in. This requires discipline, the ability to say no to purchasing items we have not budgeted for, to stick to our plan.

Forming the circle is a way of developing a spending plan of a budget - an essential tool to plan your financial life, together with God! For Christians, a spending plan is a spiritual tool that reminds us whose money we are managing. God uses money as a tool, a test and a testimony. A tool to accomplish His purposes, a test of our faithfulness as a steward and a testimony to Gods faithfulness in providing and guiding.

The circle is simply a way of portioning the income you receive, according to three main categories – your obligations, your needs and your wants.

Your obligations are fixed costs, which are generally the same each month and easy to plan. These encompass such spending as mortgage or rent, water and energy, insurances and subscriptions.

Your needs are variable expenses such as food, small items of clothing, personal care and entertainment.

Your wants are larger purchases which you need to save for, like furniture, house maintenance, car expenses, vacations.

Money is always on its way somewhere. What you do with it while it is in your keeping and the direction you send it in say much

about you. Your treatment of and respect for money, how you make it, and how you spend it, reflects your character.
From this analysis, the goal is to define a lifestyle and then begin to invest, give away any surplus to others in need or where the Lord directs. A defined lifestyle gives us FREEDOM to more intimately pursue the Lord and be engaged in His purposes. This journey is one of moving from "Chaos to Order" and requires self-control, discipline and will-power.

Each person will have a different circle according to your circumstances, your responsibilities and your plans. Each slice of the pie, or circle is not necessarily the same size as depicted here. This illustration is only meant to show the idea of a circle of the main categories to spend or invest your income.

> How Big is your Circle?

We have now defined what is in our circles, now we will briefly look at how big is our circle. Often we think that my problems would go away if I just had a little more money – increase our income. Well that may reduce some short- term issues, yet it does not address the real issue which we have already considered – how much is enough?

How big is the size of your circle? This is a question we must have a conviction on. We undoubtedly will come to the conclusion that more will not bring more satisfaction.

If the obligations, needs and desires are not defined – then we will suffer an overflow of desires which will necessitate enlarging our circle ... which means our lifestyle is constantly expanding and must be financed by even more money.

There are consequences.
There will be no overflow, money to bless God and others because all is being used up ...
If circumstances change (loss of job, divorce, serious illness etc.), then you won't have enough money to finance the larger circle.

> Is Your Circle Closed?

We now come to the real issue – have we put a limit or cap on our debts, what we need, and what we desire. This is what it means to close your circle. It will take willpower and conviction to limit your lifestyle.

Read the following quote by James Dobson. It puts things into perspective.

"I have concluded that the accumulation of wealth, even if I could achieve it, is an insufficient reason for living. When I reach the end of my days, a moment or two from now I must look backward on something more meaningful than the pursuit of houses, land, machines, stocks and bonds. Nor is fame any lasting benefit. I will consider my earthly existence to have been wasted unless I can recall a loving family, a consistent investment in the lives of people and an earnest attempt to serve the God who made me. Nothing else makes much sense."   James Dobson, Jr.

The Lord distributes the worlds good, our strengths, and our talents with inequality in order be moved to dependence upon the Lord. This dependence is known as FAITH and it will take faith to live peacefully and freely in reference to these questions.

Read again Hebrews 11:6,

*"And without faith it is impossible to please Him, for
he who comes to God must believe that He is and that
He is a rewarder of those who seek Him."*

The Lord is calling you to a deeper walk with Him through the actual handling of your money and finances. Reflect on what you are learning and how you are growing in the Lord.

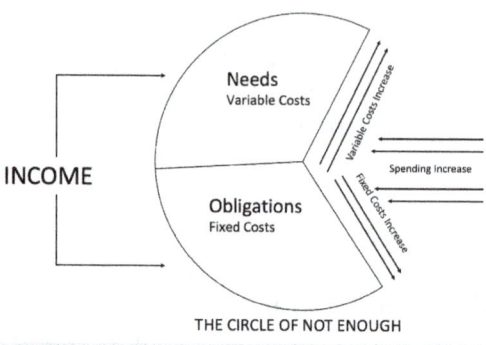

THE CIRCLE OF NOT ENOUGH

If a limit on spending is not set, our circle will be an 'open circle.' When you are constantly focused on desires, on buying more and more, the circle expands. A consequence is that whatever comes in, goes out. Spending increases, due to the need to finance an ever-increasing lifestyle.

> Closing the Circle

Here we introduce the concept of 'Closing Your Circle.' This means to limit your expenditure by making a plan, in prayer, together with God and, if appropriate, your partner. In 'Closing Your Circle' you say, "Lord, if you will provide what we have agreed, then that is enough for me to all you are asking me to do. I thank you with what you are providing, and I will be content with that. If you give me more, than I will not spend it all on myself, but use the excess I receive to bless my family and extend your Kingdom.

On the basis that God owns it all... I have to ask tough questions. "Lord, what do you want me to do with your money?" "Lord, how much of your money should I spend on myself?"
Once I have made my spending plan and my income has been apportioned into the various categories according to my priorities, closing the circle means to stop spending any more in all those categories.

> An overflowing Circle

Jesus stated very clearly that the measure by which He can trust us with what He called, " True riches" will be determined by how faithful we are in using the money He has entrusted us with. True riches encompass 'treasures in heaven', an intimate relationship with Christ, and an abundant life. He also stated that giving would lead to abundance. "give, and it will be given to you. Good measure, pressed down, shaken together, running over, will be put into your lap. For with the measure you use it will be measured back to you." (Luke 6:38)

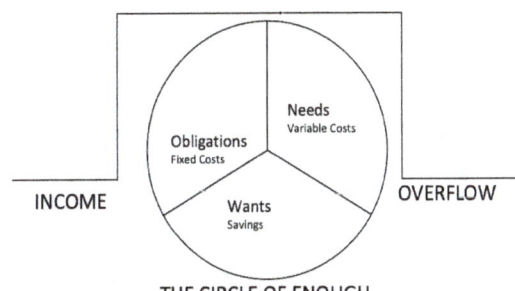

THE CIRCLE OF ENOUGH

The Lord will not release this abundance, if it is going to be spent on an ever-increasing lifestyle. It will be released when we limit spending on ourselves and use the abundance to bless others.

Financial success is so simple. Spend less than you earn over a long period of time and you will be financially successful! Sounds simple, but not so easy to put into practice! When my circle is closed, then I can start asking the Lord for overflow!

Overflow can be achieved in two ways. First of all, by earning more. Secondly, by reducing my spending. Earning more is generally much more difficult to achieve than spending less! If my circle is closed, then any income which I do not need for the three areas flows over.

A spending plan paints an accurate picture of our finances: we know how much is coming in and how much is going out. This may seem obvious, but millions spend more than they earn each month.

It helps us make informed choices about our spending: we are able to make the difficult trade-offs in our choices which are harder to make in the heat of the moment.

A spending plan establishes priorities: by making us focus on our priority payments, those items which carry a penalty for non-payment (e.g. income tax, debt) and those items which really do matter to us, such as saving for our car (repairs), a wedding anniversary or a holiday.

It makes money go further: because good planning resists casual spending and anticipates problems while there is time to address them or make adjustments.

A spending plan helps us reach our life goals, puts us back in control of our finances and helps us on the road to finding "financial freedom".

For Christians, it is a spiritual tool for Christians which reminds us whose money we are managing.

Chapter 6 -
Learning Contentment

"Contentment is the only real wealth."
Alfred Nobel (founder of Nobel Prize)

"He is not fool to lose what he can not keep
to gain what he can not lose."
Jim Elliot

As we can attain order in our finances we find, first, freedom and then, peace but these do not necessarily bring happiness and joy. Happiness and joy are only a product of being content no matter how much wealth and resources we have. Contentment doesn't mean you are happy in the bad times. It means you are satisfied with life because you know that God has things in control.

Note the following definition of contentment: Contentment is a mental or emotional state of satisfaction drawn from being at ease in one's situation, body and mind. Contentment is a state of having accepted one's situation and results in happiness.

Jesus tells the following story with a simple message, our lives are not to be filled with the riches of this world and all of its greed for possessions and power. Our lives are to be rich toward God in addition, we will have to give an account of our actions. We will answer before the Lord what we have done with what we have been given. Contentment is the critical step in living this out.

"He said to them, "Beware, and be on your guard against every form of greed; for not even when one has an abundance does his life consist of his possessions." And He told them a parable, saying, "The land of a rich man was very productive. And he began reasoning to himself, saying, 'What shall I do, since I have no place to store my crops?' Then he said, 'This is what I will do: I will tear down my barns and build larger ones, and there I will store all my grain and my goods. And I will say to my soul, "Soul, you have many goods laid up for many years to come; take your ease, eat, drink and be merry."' But God said to him, 'You fool! This very night your soul is required of you; and now who will own what you have prepared?' So is the man who stores up treasure for himself, and is not rich toward God." (Luke 12:15-21)

Principles on Contentment

We will examine seven principles on contentment and how to be content. Let's first read several verses that reference being content.

> *"Make sure that your character is free from the love of money, being content with what you have; for He Himself has said, "I will never desert you, nor will I ever forsake you," (Hebrews 13:5)*

> *"He who loves money will not be satisfied with money, nor he who loves wealth with his income; this also is vanity.." (Proverbs 5:9)*

> *"Give me neither poverty nor riches; feed me with the food that is needful for me, lest I be full and deny you and say, "Who is the Lord?" or lest I be poor and steal and profane the name of my God..." (Proverbs 30:8,9)*

1. Contentment at its core is an issue of control and results. 1 Chronicles 29:11-12
2. Contentment requires an eternal rather than a temporal perspective of life. We exchange temporal wealth for eternal reward. Matthew 6:19-21

3. The secret about contentment is that it can be learned.
    Philippians 4:8-13
4. Life is not found in our possessions but in Christ alone. Life is
    about gift and grace.
    Luke 12:51, Col 3:4, John 10:10, Philippians 1:21
5. Godliness with contentment is a means of great gain.
    1 Timothy 6:6
6. The pursuit of contentment is a spiritual challenge and we all
    will have to give an account.
    1 Corinthians 3
7. Contentment is more than freedom, it frees us from worry in
    order to serve, build relationships and bless others.
    Galatians 5:13

1. Contentment at its core is an issue of Control and Result

We previously looked at 1 Chronicles 29:11-12 from which we
understand that God owns it all. We also concluded that the Lord
is in control and the overseer of the results in this world. If we embrace this fact we can rest in the character and grace of the Lord.
Resting in the Lord is tantamount to being content.

Psalms 23:1 says
   "The Lord is my shepherd; I shall not want."
David wrote this Psalm. You can hear the contentment in his voice
because he knows that he will never be left wanting. God is the
shepherd and we are the sheep. God will take care of His sheep
and we need to trust in His promises.
   " Come to me all you who are weary and heavy laden
   and I will give you rest." (Matthew 11:28-29)

We also find a great promise in Philippians 4:19 –
   "And my God will supply every need of yours accord-
   ing to his riches in glory in Christ Jesus."

Contentment helps us answer these questions:
                    How much is enough?
Who controls the flow of all things into my life?
Does God have my best interests at heart?
How do I respond to suffering and difficulties?

Ken Boa speaks to the issue of contentment.

"The real issue of contentment is whether it is Christ or ourselves who determine the content (e.g., money, position, family, circumstances) of our lives. When we seek to control the content, we inevitably turn to the criterion of comparison to measure what it should look like. The problem is that comparison is the enemy of contentment— there will always be people who possess a greater quality or quantity of what we think we should have. Because of this, comparison leads to covetousness. Instead of loving our neighbors, we find ourselves loving what they possess. Covetousness in turn leads to a competitive spirit. We find ourselves competing with others for the limited resources to which we think we are entitled. Competition often becomes a vehicle through which we seek to authenticate our identity or prove our capability. This kind of competition tempts us to compromise our character. When we want something enough, we may be willing to steamroll our convictions in order to attain it. We find ourselves cutting corners, misrepresenting the truth, cheating, or using people as objects to accomplish our self-driven purposes. It is only when we allow Christ to determine the content of our lives that we can discover the secret of contentment. Instead of comparing ourselves with others, we must realize that the Lord alone knows what is best for us and loves us enough to use our present circumstances to accomplish eternal good. We can be content when we put our hope in His character rather than our own concept of how our lives should appear."

2. Contentment requires an eternal rather than a temporal perspective of life.

This temporal life will determine my eternity and its condition. My reward is found in only heaven. We need to take hold of this idea found in Matthew 6:21, "Where my treasure is where my heart is." Our hearts are only satisfied with the things of the eternal

3. The secret about contentment is that it can be learned.

*"Not that I am speaking of being in need, for I have
learned in whatever situation I am to be content.
I know how to be brought low, and I know how
to abound. In any and every circumstance, I have
learned the secret of facing plenty and hunger, abundance and need. I can do all things through Him who
strengthens me." (Philippians 4:11-13)*

Paul really drives home the main point of contentment in these
three verses. "I am to be content" means that there is a prede-
termined attitude for all situations. It is planned and through
self-discipline it can be achieved. Paul's statement that "I can do
all things through Him who strengthens me" must be engraved in
our hearts and minds. When we focus on the Word, we can respond appropriately in all circumstances. Christ is our Savior and
Lord. He won't let us down. He will strengthen us to be content.

4. Life is not found in our possessions but in Christ alone. He is our life.

*"And he said to them, 'take care, and be on your guard
against all covetousness, for one's life does not consist
in the abundance of his possessions.'" (Luke 12:15)*

Coveting is the opposite of contentment. If jealousy of others
pushes you to getting things that they have then you are missing
the point. Jesus said "life does not consist in the abundance of
his possessions." Don't be swayed by the glamour and prestige
around you. It is all an attempt by Satan to keep you worldly
minded and not eternally minded.

*"For the sake of Christ, then, I am content with weak-
nesses, insults, hardships, persecutions, and calami-
ties. For when I am weak, then I am strong."
(2 Corinthians 12:10)*

There is an important point here: "for the sake of Christ." This
is the reason why we all can be content. Christ left perfection in
Heaven to come down to the most disorderly place ever. He came
down willingly, knowing that men would lead Him to a horrific

death on a cross, so that we could be saved and be holy before God. That is why we can be content in all of the bad stuff. If Christ loved us enough to die for us all, then being content is nothing compared to the gift we have been given. We can be thankful in all things because Christ loved us all of the way to the cross.

If your full trust is in the Lord then you can be assured that His promises are true. God will never leave nor forsake you. Therefore, there is no need to fret. God has planned out every day of your life, so ask Him for guidance and allow Him to lead you.

Contentment begins with and in our relationship with Jesus Christ. John 10:10 The thief comes only to steal and kill and destroy; I came that they may have life, and have it abundantly."

Note the idea we have been given magnificent promises in 2 Peter 1:2-4, "Grace and peace be multiplied to you in the knowledge of God and of Jesus our Lord; seeing that His divine power has granted to us everything pertaining to life and godliness, through the true knowledge of Him who called us by His own glory and excellence. For by these He has granted to us His precious and magnificent promises, so that by them you may become partakers of the divine nature

Finally we in obedience and possess an overflowing gratitude. Colossians 2:6-7,
> *"Therefore as you have received Christ Jesus the Lord, so walk in Him, having been firmly rooted and now being built up in Him and established in your faith, just as you were instructed, and overflowing with gratitude."*

5. Godliness with contentment is a means of great gain.

"But Godliness with contentment is great gain, for we brought nothing into the world, and we cannot take anything out of the world. But if we have food and clothing, with these we will be content."
(1 Timothy 6:6-8)

We experience great gain in our heart, now and in eternity, when we exercise contentment with Godliness. The world is out for gain: cars, houses, fame, etc.... Timothy is conveying that we need to be satisfied with what we have. Not that cars, houses and fame are bad, but if we are pushing for these kinds of things then there may be a heart issue with contentment that needs to be looked at. And as Timothy said, "we cannot take anything out of the world." Why strive so hard for material things that mean nothing in the end?

6. The pursuit of contentment is a spiritual battle

Pursuing contentment is a spiritual battle in which we will have opposition from the world and the devil. It will not be easy. We also will have to die to our flesh and meeting its desires and wants. We must be careful not to be too busy, as this will rob us of joy and contentment. We live in the constant pressure and temptation of the enemy to pursue gain things and being defined by things and people. There is no let up.

7. Contentment is more than freedom.

Order frees us from worry SO we may exercise maturity to serve and bless others. Contentment is not just For us, it is a state where we can help others. See Galatians 5:13,
"For you were called to freedom, brethren; only do not turn your freedom into an opportunity for the flesh, but through love serve one another."

Matthew 6:25-26,
"Therefore I tell you, do not be anxious about your life, what you will eat or what you will drink, nor about your body, what you will put on. Is not life more than food, and the body more than clothing? Look at the birds of the air: they neither sow nor reap nor gather into barns, and yet your Heavenly Father feeds them. Are you not of more value than they?"

Worry is also the complete opposite of contentment. God loves us. He will take care of us. When you worry about things, you are not putting your full trust in God.

When we are in a frenzied pursuit for material things we will never find contentment. Many Christians get sucked into the swamp of discontent. Are you a contented Christian? Think over this past week: Was your time spent pursuing godliness with contentment, or was it consumed with going after material things? I'm not talking about the basics--food, clothing, and shelter. I'm talking about a lifestyle marked by the pursuit of all of the junk that Madison Avenue tries to convince us that we need.

The Secret of Contentment

"We want a whole race perpetually in pursuit of the rainbow's end, never honest, nor kind, nor happy now, but always using as mere fuel wherewith to heap the altar of the future every real gift which is offered them in the Present." Dr. Ken Boa.

Uncle Screwtape's diabolical counsel to his nephew Wormwood in C. S. Lewis' The Screwtape Letters is a reminder that most of us live more in the future than in the present.

"Somehow we think that the days ahead will make up for what we perceive to be our present lack. We think, When I get this or when that happens, then I'll be happy," but this is an exercise in self-deception that overlooks the fact that even when we get what we want, it never delivers what it promised.

Most of us don't know precisely what we want, but we are certain we don't have it. Driven by dissatisfaction, we pursue the treasure at the end of the rainbow and rarely drink deeply at the well of the present moment, which is all we ever have. The truth is that if we are not satisfied with what we have, we will never be satisfied with what we want. As we learn the secret of contentment, we will be less impressed by numbers, less driven to achieve, less hurried, and more alive to the grace of the present moment.

Practicing Simplicity

A key practice in becoming and living in contentment is to live a life of simplicity. We live in complex times with technology and the speed in which we get around and it can be overwhelming. To be content is live free from the things of this world that entangle us illustrated by the soldier in 2 Timothy 2:4.

There is an insight about living in simplicity in 2 Corinthians 11:3, *"But I am afraid that, as the serpent deceived Eve by his craftiness, your minds will be led astray from the simplicity and purity of devotion to Christ."*

Complexity and having more is a deception of the enemy. We think we own and have things that make life better, in reality the things own us because we have to manage them and look after them. Life with complexity maybe quicker but it is not better.

How can you simplify your life? Give old stuff away and downsize. You will be amazed when the "space" of your life is free from stuff and then filled with the Lord and people.

Four Barriers to Pursuing Contentment

Contentment is not easy to achieve and hard to maintain. There are four things that will block us or will eat away at contentment like a cancer. These simply are:
1. Competing, 2. Comparing, 3. Counting, 4. Controlling.

Competition is when we use other people to lift us or that we try to get our identify needs meet by winning and or outdoing someone else. We are implored to compete to win the prize, yet that is competing with ourselves to do our best.
Comparing is the devil's game to tell us that we need more, or we are not as good as someone else because they have more. Counting is good in that we need accurate numbers and understanding where we are financially, yet when we count to prove our self worth or as a scorecard of self made progress, the results will be disaster.
Controlling people or a situation is only an opportunity for the flesh to rise up and be in charge. Watch out for these 4 C's!!

The Law of Diminishing Returns

There is a principle in economics that also applies to life and our pursuit of contentment, that is the "Law of Diminishing Returns". This principle is defined by "a point at which the level of profits or benefits gained is less than the amount of money or energy invested."

The Law of Diminishing Returns could be illustrated by what I call the Fulfilment Curve.
If we plot fulfilment against money spent, we see first a sharp rise in fulfilment with the ability to spend to meet basic needs.
The curve continues to rise as we spend on basic comforts. However, as we transition into spending more on luxuries, the return on our extra spending tails off as we move into consumerism. But consumerism adds little to our fulfilment and wellbeing as well as being disastrous for the planet.

Looking at the sociological and psychological consequences of our all-consuming epidemic, Tim Kasser argues, "It's a particular strand of overconsumption, where we purchase things, not to fulfil our basic needs, but when we use stuff to fill some voids about our lives and make social statements about ourselves. Our obsessive relationship with material things is actually jeopardising our relationships, which have proven over and over to be the biggest determining factor in our happiness once our basic needs are met."

LAW OF DIMINISHING RETURNS

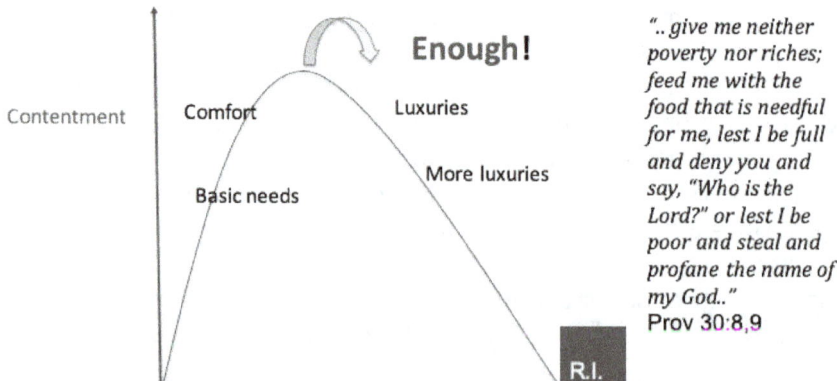

Contentment

Comfort

Enough!

Luxuries

More luxuries

Basic needs

R.I.

Spending

".. give me neither poverty nor riches; feed me with the food that is needful for me, lest I be full and deny you and say, "Who is the Lord?" or lest I be poor and steal and profane the name of my God.."
Prov 30:8,9

Yet there is a point that when we accumulate more or begin to seek after luxuries our contentment diminishes, it goes down, The more we have the less we are content.

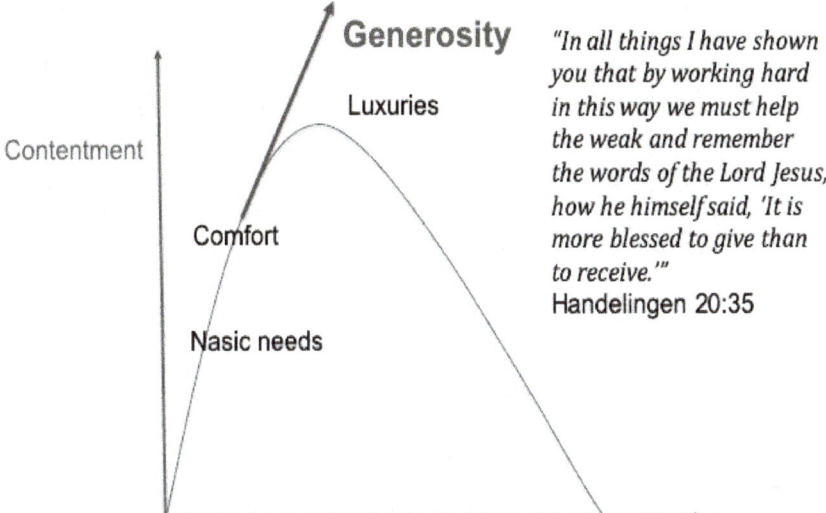

Generosity

Luxuries

Contentment

Comfort

Nasic needs

"In all things I have shown you that by working hard in this way we must help the weak and remember the words of the Lord Jesus, how he himself said, 'It is more blessed to give than to receive.'"
Handelingen 20:35

The only way to grow in contentment is at the point of enjoying what we have been entrusted with we begin to generously give the excess away.
Generosity is the only path to continually grow in contentment.
Generosity is the subject of the next stop on the road.

How to Survive in a Financial Crisis

Sometimes we find ourselves in a financial crisis, Here are ten steps to consider when you are in a financial crisis.

1. Absolutely, positively, do not increase your present level of consumer debt. No more credit cards, no matter what. Stop buying non-essentials. Cut back on optional lifestyle spending. Place a priority on your mortgage payment and various insurance premiums.
2. Run toward your creditors, not away from them. Contact each one, explaining your budget situation and how much you have available. Be realistic. Show them a list of your other creditors, and how you are dividing your available money among them. Once you've made a promise to them, honor it at all cost.
3. Think twice before putting your house up for sale. The cost of

real estate commissions, moving, and replacement housing often adds up to more than you're presently paying. Contact your mortgage lender. They will generally work with people who display a responsible attitude. Ask for partial payments for a time, or to extend the loan to lower the monthly payment..

4. Raise cash by selectively selling assets. Every house is filled with items that are no longer used but in good condition. Advertise in "bargain mart"-type classified newspapers or online. Bicycles, boats, electronic and computer items sell quickly if priced right. If you have investments to sell, first sell the ones in which you have a loss. You can often use losses to offset your other income and reduce income tax obligations.

5. Borrow from your life insurance. Policies that build cash values allow you to borrow up to the "surrender value." If you don't pay it back (or die while the loan is still unpaid), the amount of insurance paid to your beneficiary will be reduced by the amount of the loan.

6. Borrow from the college fund. This is a decision for the whole family. If college is years away, you can work on replenishing the fund after your debt crisis is over. If college is coming up soon, your child might qualify for financial aid and government loans.

7. To conserve cash, temporarily stop funding your retirement plans. While many company plans allow you to borrow against your vested benefit, we would advise against it. This is truly a "last resort" measure.

8. Once a bill is paid off, don't reduce your debt-retirement budget. Take the money that you were using on that bill and put it toward your remaining highest interest rate debt.

9. Avoid bankruptcy. This should not be considered an option. It is a matter of personal and Christian integrity to pay your debts in full. The stigma of bankruptcy stays with you a long time and could affect future applications for employment and housing for years.

Practical Application

Practice being thankful in every situation.
Start a Journal of praise and thanksgiving.

Chapter 7 - Being generous

"Generosity is what keeps the things we own from owning us."
Eugene Cho

"Do all the good you can, by all the means you can, in all the ways you can, in all the places you can, at all the times you can, to all the people you can, as long as ever you can."
John Wesley

We are Blessed to be a Blessing

We have been blessed with many spiritual gifts and treasures, but they are not for yourself. We are to be conduits (branches) for God to work through to bear much fruit which includes the fruit of the spirit: love, joy, peace, patience, kindness, goodness, faith, meekness and self-control. We have been given (blessed with) these fruits in order to reflect the love of the Lord, to grow, and minister to others. We are called to do this generously.

The Power of Generosity

Generosity is an attribute with many great qualities: being generous has a power associated with it, generosity is attractive to others, it grows and extends to people's lives, and it expands God's Kingdom. We see this in Jesus' parable of the "Good Samaritan."

The Good Samaritan

"Jesus replied and said, "A man was going down from

Jerusalem to Jericho, and fell among robbers, and they stripped him and beat him, and went away leaving him half dead. And by chance a priest was going down on that road, and when he saw him, he passed by on the other side. Likewise a Levite also, when he came to the place and saw him, passed by on the other side. But a Samaritan, who was on a journey, came upon him; and when he saw him, he felt compassion, and came to him and bandaged up his wounds, pouring oil and wine on them; and he put him on his own beast, and brought him to an inn and took care of him. On the next day he took out two denarii and gave them to the innkeeper and said, 'Take care of him; and whatever more you spend, when I return I will repay you.' Which of these three do you think proved to be a neighbor to the man who fell into the robbers' hands?" And he said, "The one who showed mercy toward him." Then Jesus said to him, "Go and do the same." (Luke 10:30-37)

In this story of the 'Good Samaritan', we see generosity lived out even when the consequences could have been hurtful or devastating. The story shows us that we can be merciful and generous to anyone if we allow the Lord to direct us. It is a picture of God and His grace towards us.

Generosity Begins with the Lord and Reflects His Heart

God's is very generous with us: unlimited and forever forgiveness {past, present, and future), unconditional love, the riches of an eternal life, and the fruit of spirit. His gifts are infinite, unmeasureable, and undeserved. The impact of His grace and gifts should overwhelm us and create a thirst or desire to take hold of what we possess.

Read about the depth of His love in Ephesians 3:14-19,
"For this reason I bow my knees before the Father, rom whom every family in heaven and on earth derives its name, that He would grant you, according to the riches of His glory, to be strengthened with power

through His Spirit in the inner man, so that Christ
may dwell in your hearts through faith; and that you,
being rooted and grounded in love, may be able to
comprehend with all the saints what is the breadth
and length and height and depth, and to know the love
of Christ which surpasses knowledge, that you may be
filled up to all the fullness of God. 20 Now to Him who
is able to do far more abundantly beyond all that we
ask or think, according to the power that works within
us, to Him be the glory in the church and in Christ
Jesus to all generations forever and ever. Amen."

We are Already Wealthy

Our riches in Christ make us wealthy beyond belief. We have been given unfathomable riches of being "in Christ." The following are truths that help us understand and motivate us to be generous. The following statements are in the "first person" so you can personally identify with them.

- My worth and significance are found solely in Christ (which is forever and unchanging) and not in performance or in a position.
- Because of my worth in Christ, I am free from the opinions of others while listening and learning from them.
- In this freedom from opinions, I can truly serve and love others (value and honor people).
- Because of this freedom, I can give away power or empower others.
- Because of my security in Christ, I can be process focused vs. results oriented or bottom line driven.
- "In Christ" I am free from the bondage to sin among which pride is one of the chief ones.
- His love and acceptance give me a security that helps me examine my motives and purify my motives.
- When my needs are met, I can give my life away and not try and manipulate situations or other people in order to meet those needs.

We have been brought with a price.

"You are not your own, for you were bought with a price. So glorify God in your body." You are of infinite worth in God's eyes. (1 Corinthians 6:19-20)

David Wilkerson teaches on how much we have in Christ. "Christ is the treasure chest in the field. And in Him, I've found all that I'll ever need. No more trying to find purpose in ministry. No more looking for fulfillment in family or friends. No more needing to build something for God, or to be a success, or to feel useful. No more keeping up with the crowd, or trying to prove something. No more searching for ways to please people. No more trying to think or reason my way out of difficulties.

I've found what I'm looking for. My treasure, my pearl, is Christ. And all that the Owner asks of me is, "David, I love you. Let me adopt you. I've already signed the papers with my own Son's blood. You're now a joint heir with him of everything I possess."

What a bargain. I give up my filthy rags of self-reliance and good works. I lay aside my worn-out shoes of striving. I leave behind my sleepless nights on the streets of doubt and fear. And in return, I am adopted by a King. This is what happens when you seek the pearl, the treasure, till you find him. Jesus offers you everything he is. He brings you joy, peace, purpose, holiness. And He becomes your everything—your waking, your sleeping, your morning, after-noon, and evening."

We have been an infinite storehouse of eternal treasure, yet we must receive the gift, unwrap it, and put it into practice. Other-wise it is like having all of the gifts under the Christmas tree and we leave them there unwrapped. We have been given so much that we often take grace for granted. We must never be complacent with the gifts and resources given to us.

Our Role in Being Generous

We have been blessed in order to be a blessing. Exercising gener-osity involves a whole-life generosity of all of our resources from

God's incredible gifts to our time and talent and as well as in our finances. Examine the following verses and reflect on our role in generosity.

"And if I give all my possessions to feed the poor, and if I surrender my body to be burned, but do not have love, it profits me nothing." (1 Corinthians 13:3)

"Remember the words of the Lord Jesus, that He Himself said, 'It is more blessed to give than to receive'" (Acts 20:35)

"Now this I say, he who sows sparingly will also reap sparingly, and he who sows bountifully will also reap bountifully. Each one must do just as he has purposed in his heart, not grudgingly or under compulsion, for God loves a cheerful giver. And God is able to make all grace abound to you, so that always having all sufficiency in everything, you may have an abundance for every good deed..." (2 Corinthians 9:6-8)

"There is one who scatters, and yet increases all the more, and there is one who withholds what is justly due, and yet it results only in want. The generous man will be prosperous, and he who waters will himself be watered." (Proverbs 11:24-25)

Exercising Generosity

For us to practice the power of generosity consider the following elements:

1. Foundation:

Preparation: We begin with 1 Timothy 6:17-18 as it tells us to fix our hope on the certainty of God. We need to be practicing stewardship and surrender, we need to make wise lifestyle choices with our finances to be in a position to give and do it generously. The final part of preparation is to be content with what you have been given.

2. God's Part

Possession: We receive God's infinite love, gifts, and riches through Christ and we possess it. We make it ours to enjoy and live from. Galatians 2:20
Promise: The Lord makes us a promise in 2 Corinthians 9:6-7 that if we are generous we will reap generously. God loves a cheerful giver.

3. Our Part

Practice: We need to be thankful in all things. We are asked to give and give freely
Product: Generous people are attractive. We glorify the Lord and people love to connect with us. We are a light to the world. Generous people are filled with love to give away.
Purpose: Generosity has a purpose which is to glorify the Lord, to extend God's Kingdom purposes, and make a difference in this world.

"Contrary to our culture, the biblical doctrine of grace humbles us without degrading us, and elevates us without inflating us. It tells us that apart from Christ, we have nothing and can do nothing of eternal value. We are spiritually impotent and inadequate without Him, and we must not put our confidence in the flesh (Philippians 3:3). On the other hand, grace also tells us that we have become new creatures in Christ, having been transferred from the kingdom of darkness to the kingdom of His light, life, and love. In Him, we now enjoy complete forgiveness from sins and limitless privileges as unconditionally accepted members of God's family. Our past has been changed because of our new heredity in Christ, and our future is secure because of our new destiny as members of His body." Ken Boa, Conformed to His Image

Observations about generosity and people:

- Generous people have a much better outlook on their life and

their circumstances.
- Generous people work from an attitude of abundance rather than scarcity or limitations.
- Generosity is attractive and attracts people.
- You don't need anything more in order to practice generosity.
- It is much more than giving, it is loving with no strings attached.
- It is much more than money, it is our life invested in people.
- Generosity is usually the result of our maturity in the Lord.
- We can walk with the Lord, give/tithe, have good relationships and yet, not practice generosity.
- Generosity will have eternal consequences that cannot be measured in our life times.
- The lack of generosity leads to holding on to things and eventually those things owning you.
- Ungenerous people end up becoming isolated and relationships are more like acquaintances.
- The ungenerous person tends not to trust others believing they want something from them

Generosity has a Great Blessings

Generosity will reap a reward. Note the outcomes of being generous.

1. Promises – Generosity has many promises.

"Good will come to those who are generous and lend freely, who conduct their affairs with justice. "(Psalms 112:5)

"Honor the LORD with your wealth, with the first fruits of all your crops; then your barns will be filled to overflowing, and your vats will brim over with new wine." (Proverbs 3:9, 10)

"One man gives freely, yet gains even more; another withholds unduly, but comes to poverty. A generous man will prosper; he who refreshes others will himself be refreshed." (Proverbs 11:24 - 25)

"The generous will themselves be blessed, for they share their food with the poor." (Proverbs 22:9)

" ...be generous to the poor, and everything will be clean for you." (Luke 11:41)

2. Law of the Harvest - If we sow well we will reap well.

"Do not be deceived, God is not mocked; for whatever a man sows, this he will also reap. For the one who sows to his own flesh will from the flesh reap corruption, but the one who sows to the Spirit will from the Spirit reap eternal life. Let us not lose heart in doing good, for in due time we will reap if we do not grow weary. So then, while we have opportunity, let us do good to all people, and especially to those who are of the household of the faith." (Galatians 6: 7-10)

3. You grow as you give away your life and resources.

"Feed the hungry, and help those in trouble. Then your light will shine out from the darkness, and the darkness around you will be as bright as noon." (Isaiah 58:10)

A Generosity Lifestyle

At the very center of generous living is an awareness of how precious and valuable are other people. Just as having a financial plan can help you free up more money for giving, so having a lifestyle strategy can help make generosity a reality in your life. Here are six lifestyle, action steps can help you identify and take advantage of the opportunities God gives you.

1. Begin by valuing people. People are made in the image of God and eternal beings. We need to value all by sharing the Gospel with them and/or helping them grow.

2. Examine your priorities. Start by examining your priorities, reminding yourself of the value God places on people. Think about the things that matter and put those items (or

people) at the top of your list.

3. Take an inventory your assets. Make a list of what you have to offer: your time, your talents, and your possessions. Whether we are skilled at serving, teaching, planning, leading, or something else, our job is to share our gifts with others. And just as financial resources can be managed carefully, so these assets must be used effectively to serve others. Don't waste your resources; instead, be prepared to use them when the opportunity arises.

4. Ask the right questions. When someone asks us to give our time, skills, or possessions to a particular group or cause, we often respond with the wrong questions. Instead of asking, "Is it convenient for me?" or "What do I get out of it?" start by asking whether or not God would want you to use your resources in this way.

5. Eliminate expectations. When you give time, talents, or possessions, be sure you do not expect to receive anything in return. Remember that sacrificial giving involves a cost to yourself, not a reward for your generosity.

6. Give your schedule to God. Start each day by giving your schedule – your calendar, your appointments, your plans – to God. Ask Him to show you how He wants you to use your time, and give Him the freedom to interrupt your agenda.

Lifestyle generosity doesn't happen overnight. Instead, it's more of a growth process: the more you give, the better you feel. The more joyful and content you are, the more you want to give. Begin to implement these six action steps to start your journey toward a generous life.

Practical Application

Give abundantly and anonymously to someone who is in great need.
In conversations with others, ask how you can pray for them.

Chapter 8 - Investing in Eternity

"What we do in this life, echoes in eternity!"
Maximus

"You have not lived today until you have done something for
someone who can never repay you."
John Bunyon

C.S. Lewis wrote in the "The Problem of Pain",
"Our Father refreshes us on the journey with some pleasant
inns, but will not encourage us to mistake them for home."

We are made for another world because we are spiritual beings at
our core. We are made in the image of God and God transcends
this world. We live here as guests or visitors. Heaven is our home
and destination, so don't become so comfortable in this life and
that your roots are so deep that leaving will be a tragedy.

Dinner is Served

Jesus tells the following story of the wedding feast which is a parable illustrating eternity and how we should live our lives – what
are we truly focused on.

> "Jesus spoke to them again in parables, saying, "The
> kingdom of heaven may be compared to a king who
> gave a wedding feast for his son. And he sent out his
> slaves to call those who had been invited to the wed-

ding feast, and they were unwilling to come. Again he sent out other slaves saying, 'Tell those who have been invited, "Behold, I have prepared my dinner; my oxen and my fattened livestock are all butchered and everything is ready; come to the wedding feast."' But they paid no attention and went their way, one to his own farm, another to his business, and the rest seized his slaves and mistreated them and killed them. But the king was enraged, and he sent his armies and destroyed those murderers and set their city on fire. Then he *said to his slaves, 'The wedding is ready, but those who were invited were not worthy. Go therefore to the main highways, and as many as you find there, invite to the wedding feast.' Those slaves went out into the streets and gathered together all they found, both evil and good; and the wedding hall was filled with dinner guests.

"But when the king came in to look over the dinner guests, he saw a man there who was not dressed in wedding clothes, and he said to him, 'Friend, how did you come in here without wedding clothes?' And the man was speechless. Then the king said to the servants, 'Bind him hand and foot, and throw him into the outer darkness; in that place there will be weeping and gnashing of teeth.' For many are called, but few are chosen." (Matthew 22:1-14)

Jesus is preparing His disciples with this story that in the end "many are called and few are chosen", in other words not everyone will make it into eternity or heaven. The question for us as faithful followers is 'are we fully and truly engaged in inviting all to the banquets table of the Lord?' This life is more than living in Order (stewardship and managed finances), it is actually more than Maturity (contentment and generosity).

It is all about Eternity.

Benefits of an Eternal Life over a Temporal Life

When we possess our new nature and our spirit is indwelt by the Holy Spirit, we gain many benefits and advantages that are simply not possibly as a non-believer. The following are ten such attributes that we gain:

1. Security – our security is in the unchanging Christ and not in the accolades of the world
2. Significance – our worth is based on the price God paid for us (Christ) not on our possessions or position
3. Satisfaction – our fulfillment is found in eternal things not the temporal
4. Power – our power comes from the infinite power of Christ rather than our limited resources
5. Life – we gain a life that lives on into eternity with God rather than holding on to a physical life on earth
6. Wisdom – God says He will give us His wisdom which is far greater than our own
7. Vision – vision comes from God who is beyond time and space versus our limited perspective
8. Love – we are loved unconditionally and forever by God rather than the conditional love of people
9. Wholeness – an eternal life makes us whole and we are restored to function
10. Peace – God becomes our peace because we give up control and rest in Him

People think they want pleasure, recognition, popularity, status, and power, but the pursuit of these things leads, in the final analysis, to emptiness, delusion, and foolishness. God has set eternity in our hearts (Ecclesiastes 3:11), and our deepest desires are fulfillment (love, joy, peace), reality (that which does not fade away), and wisdom (skill in living).

The only path to this true fulfillment lies in the conscious choice of God's value system over that which is offered by this world. This choice is based on trusting a Person we have not yet seen.

"And though you have not seen Him, you love Him,
and though you do not see Him now, but believe in
Him, you greatly rejoice with joy inexpressible and
full of glory, obtaining as the outcome of your faith the

salvation of your souls." 1 Peter 1:8-9.

Many wander through life without a purpose, not knowing what they are supposed to be doing. Those people find themselves unhappy most of their lives because they don't enjoy what they do because they lack a purpose. We often don't give ourselves fully to a purpose because we are afraid of all the what ifs and the false expectations that appear to be real.

Abandon your Life

As we wrap up our study on "Flourishing in Troubling Times" we conclude that we must continually 'die to self' (Luke 9:23) and 'seek the Kingdom of God' (Matthew 6:33). This is an everyday battle and we need the life of Christ in us to do so.

We Live in a World of Two Opposing Economies - God's Economy vs. Man's Economy

The bible describes that we live and work in two worlds and two different economies at the same time.

Jesus said to Pilate: "My kingdom is not of this world ..." Consider the ways in which there is a tension between the two opposing economies.

> *"Come, all you who are thirsty, come to the waters; and you who have no money, come, buy and eat! Come, buy wine and milk without money and without cost." (Isaiah 55: 1-2)*

> *"For my thoughts are not your thoughts, neither are your ways my ways," declares the LORD. "As the heavens are higher than the earth, so are my ways higher than your ways and my thoughts than your thoughts." (Isaiah 55:8-9)*

> *"No one can serve two masters. Either you will hate the one and love the other, or you will be devoted to the one and despise the other. You cannot serve both*

God and money." (Matthew 6:24)

God's economy has nothing to do with money! Money has nothing to do with the reality of true satisfaction. Mammon or the power of money competes for our allegiance and tries to destroy relationships. We sometimes ask "Why did Jesus allow Himself to be sold for money?" He allowed Himself (once and for all) to be subject to man's economy, allowing Himself to be sold and bought, so He could break right through the powers of man's economy and set us free – allowing us to come into God's economy!

Our world is marked with many of us pursing money.
"But mark this: There will be terrible times in the last days. People will be lovers of themselves, lovers of money, boastful, proud, abusive, disobedient to their parents, ungrateful, unholy, without love, unforgiving, slanderous, without self-control, brutal, not lovers of the good, treacherous, rash, conceited, lovers of pleasure rather than lovers of God—having a form of godliness but denying its power. Have nothing to do with them." (2 Timothy 3:1-3)

" The Pharisees, who loved money, heard all this and were sneering at Jesus. He said to them, "You are the ones who justify yourselves in the eyes of others, but God knows your hearts. What people value highly is detestable in God's sight." (Luke 16:14)

Money will not protect us from problems --- Ecclesiastes. 5:10 "As goods increase, so do those who consume them. And what benefit are they to the owners except to feast their eyes on them?" Money will never solve financial problems ... maybe alleviate the symptoms for a short while ... financial problems are a matter of the heart.

An Eternal Perspective – Keep the Big Picture in Focus.

Our lives are but a dot on an infinite time line. We need to see that our life on earth is but a moment so we live for the eternal while in the temporal world. We then will value all of the things in this life from God's viewpoint and not man's measuring stick.

We can conclude the following: eternity gives meaning to time, our destiny defines the journey we are on, and adversity drives us to dependency.

There Is No Maturity without Ministry

For the follower of Christ, ministry is never optional—it is a calling for all believers, not merely a subset of "professionals." Laypeople bypass abundant ministry opportunities when they stumble over the assumption that if they cannot teach or preach, they are limited to vicarious ministry through their financial support of those who can. This spectator mentality causes people to overlook the God-given circumstances and abilities which they have been entrusted. All believers can be involved in some aspect of discipleship, even if this is limited to their families. No arena is insignificant, since reward is based on faithfulness to opportunity rather than the size of our ministry. We stunt our growth when we fail to serve others with eternal values at heart.

Remember and embrace the words of the Lord Jesus: "Calling them to Himself, Jesus said to them,
'You know that those who are recognized as rulers of the Gentiles lord it over them; and their great men exercise authority over them. But it is not this way among you, but whoever wishes to become great among you shall be your servant; and whoever wishes to be first among you shall be slave of all. For even the Son of Man did not come to be served, but to serve, and to give His life a ransom for many.'" (Mark 10:42-45)

Jesus' last and Great Commission given to His disciples was:
"Go therefore and make disciples of all the nations, baptizing them in the name of the Father and the Son and the Holy Spirit, teaching them to observe all that I commanded you; and lo, I am with you always, even to the end of the age." (Matthew 28:19-20)

Rewards in Heaven - We will reap a reward in eternity.

Our life on earth will affect our life in eternity. If we invest in the lives of people and do so with a right motive we will reap rewards in heaven. It is a motivator to focus on the eternal rather than the temporal. Rewards in heaven are unlimited, thus we don't compete or compare with others on the amount of rewards they receive or we receive. God will determine how they are dispensed based on our heart and motive.

Crowns - Note the crows that are available to the believer who lives with a Kingdom perspective.

"For who is our hope or joy or crown of exultation? Is it not even you, in the presence of our Lord Jesus at His coming? For you are our glory and joy."
(1 Thessalonians 2:19-20)

"And when the Chief Shepherd appears, you will receive the unfading crown of glory." (1 Peter 5:4)

"Everyone who competes in the games exercises self-control in all things. They then do it to receive a perishable wreath, but we an imperishable." (1 Corinthians 9:25)

"Blessed is a man who perseveres under trial; for once he has been approved, he will receive the crown of life which the Lord has promised to those who love Him."
(James 1:12)

"in the future there is laid up for me the crown of righteousness, which the Lord, the righteous Judge, will award to me on that day; and not only to me, but also to all who have loved His appearing." (2 Timothy 4:8)

An Eternal Perspective in the Midst of Difficulties

We briefly looked at 2 Timothy 3:1, "But realize this, that in last days difficult times will come." This was Paul's very last letter he wrote and the very last two chapters. He knew his departure was near and his time on earth was at an end. So these last two chapters hold great significance of how we are both to finish well and what is most important.

The verse says 'the last days' or it could mean 'the latter days.' As we look around our world today it is easy to see and conclude that the days in which we live are the latter days if not the last days. So what was Paul's message to Timothy – how was he to handle himself and what should his perspective be?

Paul begins by telling Timothy to "realize" the days in which he would find himself. To realize means to understand the times like the men of Issachar (1 Chronicles 12:32), see life for the reality of what is going on. We discovered this in chapter one – there is a gathering storm. In addition, Paul notes in Ephesians 5:15, "that the days are evil" – there is a spiritual battle going on. We will face difficulty, persecution, and pain. Don't despair – keep looking up.

Paul's message to Timothy was "wake up and be on guard" for the enemy crouches at the door to "kill. steal, and destroy." We need to wake up from our consuming busyness and endless distraction of entertainment to be wise and pursue the eternal. We do this by finding "hope" in the storm and by finding the hope of Christ. From the hope of Christ we then exercise faith and love.

Immediately, Paul begins to describe in 2 Timothy 3:2-9 who NOT to hang out with. He details 20 characteristics of people not to associate with such as: "holding to a form of Godliness, although they have denied its power. Avoid such men as these..."always learning and never able to come to the knowledge of the truth... so these men also oppose the truth, men of depraved mind." Bad company will tear you down and influence you to make bad decisions.

The community we surround ourselves with is critical in challenging times – Hebrews talks about "not forsaking the assembling together and all the more as we see the day drawing near." We will need the encouragement, strength, and wisdom in the battle. The enemy wants us to be alone so he can take us out. There is strength in numbers. We need the "hope of one another" – 1 Thessalonians 2:19,20. We NEED community and relationships.

Paul then instructs Timothy that he will need a committed, personal relationship with Christ which he details in (2 Timothy 3:10-17). We are to do three things. First, "Follow Him and His teaching" - "Now you followed my teaching, conduct, purpose, faith, patience, love, perseverance, persecutions, and sufferings.." Second, "Press on" knowing that ", all who desire to live godly in Christ Jesus will be persecuted." Thirdly, "Continue in the Word" - "continue in the things you have learned and become convinced of... Scripture equips us for every good work."

In the latter days we will need to "seek an intense walk of FAITH." We must seek to walk in a manner worthy of the Lord. God's word will guide our "attitude and perspective". It says in Romans 15:4 God's word is our "hope."

Then, in 2 Timothy 4:1-5 Paul instructs Timothy to
"carry on and practice ministry" - "preach the word; be ready in season and out of season... be sober in all things, endure hardship, do the work of an evangelist, fulfill your ministry."

We all have a gifting and calling which is found in our purpose. Write it out and fulfill it. Teach the truth and don't tickle the ears. We are all called to SERVE in an intentional ministry in the problems – it takes our focus off of ourselves and it actually helps others. Be engaged in sharing Christ in the trials because that is when people are open. The bottom-line is to know your purpose and calling. Examine Ephesians 2:10 and Matthew 5:16.

The fourth principle Paul gives to Timothy is "persevere and complete your mission – have a kingdom perspective"
"Fight the good fight, Finish the course, keep the faith ...In The future there is laid up for me the crown of righteousness... to all who have loved His appearing." (2 Timothy 4:6-8; 16-18)

The Lord will stand with you when all else will fall away. Glorify the Lord in your life , press on in spite of the difficulties.

When we keep looking for the 2nd coming of Christ there will be a hope and vision that comes with it. Let this guide your perspective and thus your activity. Keep focused on the Kingdom not on the externals. Night is closing in don't go to sleep. Be prepared and on alert.

Paul then shares a final personal note of God's amazing love and strength. He calls us to overcome.

"Christ stood with me and strengthened me, so that through me the proclamation might be fully accomplished, and that all the Gentiles might hear; and I was rescued out of the lion's mouth. 18 The Lord will rescue me from every evil deed, and will bring me safely to His heavenly kingdom;" (2 Timothy 4:16-18)

We are not alone –Christ lives in and through us. He will stand with us, strengthen us, accomplish His work, rescue us, bring us safely to the Kingdom.

The Ministry is about People

Being generous will tangibly impact others in both practical and spiritual ways. We are called to serve the least, the last, and the lost. The practical expression of being generous will be focused on serving and helping people. We give to God's plan which is always about people. This is the picture of Christ dying for each of us. He died not just to take away sins, but to provide a way for people to be back in relationship to God Himself.

We must be disciples to make disciples. The more we know Christ, the better we can make Him known. When Paul told the Corinthians "I determined to know nothing among you except Jesus Christ, and Him crucified" (1 Corinthians 2:2), he saw himself as a messenger who was sent to introduce the people of Corinth to a Person with whom he had an intimate relationship. He wanted them to be more impressed with Jesus than they were with him, but this required a personal introduction to Jesus, not a list of His attributes. We must know Christ as a Person before we can guide others to this level of spiritual intimacy.

We are all called to be a light in our arenas of influence. It is not optional and in fact, we are always a witness whether we like it or not because people will be watching. Thus we need to be intentional and be prepared to give an answer.

Mission – Share the Gospel Because People Need the Lord

We are called to be active in living among the "lost". The Lord has placed each of us in a special and unique setting – a family, a community, and workplace. How the Lord can use you as a light in that context?

> *"Let your light shine before men in such a way they may see your good works and glorify your father who is in heaven." The good works includes caring, listening and learning not fixing, telling or pushing an agenda. (Matthew 5:16)*

> *"In Christ is life and the life is the light of men." The believers in the group have Christ living in them. He is the life and this life is a light to others. (John 1:4,6)*

> *The King will answer and say to them, 'Truly I say to you, to the extent that you did it to one of these brothers of Mine, even the least of them, you did it to Me." (Matthew 24:40)*

Christ had a passion and a compassion to reach the lost. Paul indicated in 1 Corinthians 9:19-23 that he became all things to all men the he might save some. His heart and conviction was not just preach the gospel or share Christ with the "lost" but rather to live among the lost - to be there for them. To develop meaningful relationships with them in such a way that questions would arise.

Pray for opportunities to share your story of faith. Our faith journey in the area of finances can be one of the best ways to start a conversation with a seeker. Ask the Lord to open doors and for people to see a difference in your life and what is our hope.
> *"but sanctify Christ as Lord in your hearts, always being ready to make a defense to everyone who asks you*

to give an account for the hope that is in you, yet with gentleness and reverence;" (1 Peter 3:15)

Determine to Finish Well

Finally, are you committed to finishing your life well? Put your hand to endeavors that extend God's Kingdom. The following are ten keys to finish well. It is not easy, yet can be obtained if one is faithful.

1. A white-hot passion and a growing, intimate relationship with the Lord – Christ as life, exercising the spiritual disciplines, ministry to God, worship, and praise.
2. A humble spirit – know your strengths and weaknesses. Always be thankful in everything.
3. Healthy relationships with spouse and family – resolving conflict, emotions, care.
4. Be a part of a community with humble, broken believers.
5. A simple lifestyle – be debt free, not entangled or in slavery to money, practice contentment, and practice enjoyment.
6. A way of life that demonstrates God's ownership and our stewardship that grows into a radical generosity focused on living God's purposes of helping others. Life is not about you.
7. A clear sense of purpose and calling that leads you to priorities, margin, and wise decisions.
8. Being other centered by engaging in a ministry of discipleship and evangelism.
9. Continue to be a learner – read, learn new things, engage your mind and heart.
10. Keep focused on God's kingdom – God at work, spiritual battles and the Second Coming. Eternal vs. temporal. Biblical perspective of life.

Commitment: Pray for the lost around you. Ask the Lord to open a door to share your hope.

Conclusion—Answering God's Call

"I have found a desire within myself that no experience in this world can satisfy; the most probable explanation is that I was made for another world."
C.S. Lewis

"Having a purpose is the difference between making a living and making a life."
Tom Thiss

Man is forever searching for purpose in his life here on earth. This drive for significance is felt by all people, particularly the Christian. Beginning in Genesis and sweeping through to Revelation, we see how God has created us for a purpose. He asks each of us to look beyond our existence on earth and calls us to join Him in a relationship and in His work that is eternal. God wants a relationship with us that is intimate, growing, and obedient. It is a relationship that ministers to back God not just looking For what is in it for ourselves.

This relationship is initiated by God through His calling us to Himself. This relationship has been established through Creation, the Cross, and the Second Coming. Once grounded in this relationship, God asks us to be about His purposes in whatever context we find ourselves. Our understanding of our calling will affect our view of work, money, relationships, and ministry.

What is a calling? Calling is an invitation or summons from God to a relationship with Himself. We are called by God, to God, and for God, this beginning is all about a relationship. What we do and where we do it is our secondary calling. These are the arenas where we live out this intimate relationship with God.

For our discussion we will examine this secondary calling in two ways:

    1. A "universal" calling for all Christians - chiefly participating in God's purposes of evangelism and discipleship

    2. An "individual" calling to every Christian which includes our work, gifts, etc.

We all live in today's world but our hearts are longing for either the temporal world or the eternal Kingdom. The question is "What kingdom or world are you living for?" A Kingdom focus will give us perspective for daily living and it is this perspective that helps us flourish.

God is calling us to live in His Kingdom and He calls us to "flourish in troubling times." He will bear fruit in and through us if we will surrender and choose to become faithful stewards. We need to make wise lifestyle choices and then practice maturity by being content and generous all the while investing in eternity.

As we review the stages in the journey (Chaos-Order-Maturity-Eternity) we see the word "COME" as an overall framework. Jesus is calling us to "come" at each of these stages and there is a corresponding outcome that helps us to flourish.

God is always "Calling" us to a relationship, to His purposes and to a context where we live out our eternal life in Him.

The chart on the next page will describe the framework of the journey of C-O-M-E.

The COME Framework

The primary call of God is when He calls us into a relationship with Himself. God pursues us in order to have a love relationship with us. God always initiates this relationship with man, never the other way around.

This relationship is man's most necessary requirement for life and should be characterized by intimacy and not casualness. It must become our highest priority.

Stage	Reference	Verse	Outcome	Call of God
C – Chaos	John 7:37-39	"If any man is thirsty let him come to me and drink and from his inner most being shall flow rivers of living water."	Drink Overflowing with living water	Called to Him in salvation
O - Order	Matthew 11:38-39	"Come to me all of you who are weary and heavy laden and I will give you rest."	Rest	Called to know Him as our Life
M - Maturity	Luke 9:23	"If anyone wishes to come after me, let him deny himself take up his cross daily and follow me."	Guidance	Called to pursue His purposes
E - Eternity	Matthew 4:19	"Come follow me and I will make you fishers of men."	Legacy of men	Called to minister in the context He places us

This relationship is characterized in terms such as a child of God (John 1:12), a friend of Christ (John 15:14) and the bride of Christ, as well as brother All these characteristics are relational and yet capture different elements of what a relationship with God might be.

At the heart of each of these relationships is love. A two-way love: an unconditional love of God toward us with a command to love God in return with all of our heart, soul, might and strength (Matthew 22:37). From our part, this kind of love must be our first priority and requires all that we have - it must be total. focus Our calling to love God needs to transcend all other relationships such that they appear as hate! (Luke 14:26). What a radical call.

This relationship with God can be strengthened through the spiritual disciplines of prayer, silence, solitude, death to self, and study of God's word. The fundamental mark of a love for God is obedience (John 14:21). Obedience is at the heart of calling. We are invited to be with God and obedience is our first step. This relational calling is not just an emotional response but one of obedience.

As we see in the chart there are levels to our calling: to Him, to wholeness, to others, and to the Gospel.

A Biblical Framework For Answering God's Call

Paul teaches the people in Ephesus about who we are and how we fit into God's plan, "For we are His workmanship, created in Christ Jesus for good works, which God prepared beforehand so that we would walk in them." Ephesians 2:10. The following outlines four part to the call with some identified guidelines for each.

1. "For we are His workmanship"
   God has a plan, purpose. We fit into His plan
   God knows us, formed us, designed us, and given us passion, personality – Ps 139
2. "created in Christ Jesus"
   Intimacy, Identity, Indwelling frame who we are which directs the doing. Col 1:27-29
   We work "FROM Him" which precedes" FOR Him". Christ is our hope.
3. "for good works, which God prepared beforehand"
   we are to serve and help others, we extend God's Kingdom, and glorify Him. We join God.
   Light will shine in darkness, God has it planned and works through us.
4. "so that we would walk in them."
   We carry out God's plan. It is a journey and process,
   Purpose is far beyond a job and career.

We all seek to live lives of meaning and purpose. Only when we have a clear purpose can we set priorities and make wise choice. At the end of each of our days, our purpose will be clear - we will have given our lives in exchange for something. We may have been very intentional about this or haphazard. The challenge we all face is - what should that purpose be?

Application

An exercise that truly helps everyone live out their calling or purpose is to put it in writing. Writing out your life purpose takes time and focus. It will yield supernatural outcomes if one does it.

The most critical component in the process of discerning our unique purpose is prayer. We would do well to persist in asking God to clarify the vision of our calling, since we will never be able to discover it on our own. Begin taking action by asking key questions:

OUTCOMES "Begin with the End in Mind." Select key constituents or audiences that matter to you : i.e. God, spouse, children, parents, colleagues, and friends. Ask yourself the question, "How do I want to remembered?" Visualize your own funeral. What are your dreams? We all have dreams and aspirations.

Let us endeavor so to live that when we come to die even the undertaker will be sorry." Mark Twain

PRIORITIES Next identify and prioritize your "life accounts." What is most important? What are God's priorities and purposes that will help frame your priorities

RESOURCES What are your spiritual gifts, skills, temperaments, personality, passions?

ACTION PLANS

In your Life Plan, you create an Action Plan for each account. This is where you think through where
you are and where you want to be.

1. Purpose Statement: This is where you state what your purpose is for each account.
2. Envisioned Future: This is where you describe how the account looks when you have a "positive net worth
3. Life Verse: chose a verse that will guide you and give you perspective about life today and for the rest of life.
4. Current Reality: Now it's time to be brutally honest. Where are you in relationship to your Envisioned Future?
5. Commitment: Where you specifically commit to certain actions in order to move from your Current Reality to your Envisioned Future.

Begin by writing out the answers to these questions. Remember these were developed over a period of time, re-evaluated periodically, refined and updated. So, just start simply.

A Final Charge

We have covered a lot of ground on this journey to being all that God made you to be and to discern what He has in store for you. Be encouraged that the Lord is on the throne, He has not taken His eye off of you and He truly wants the best for you. The Lord has blessed us with Christ as our life and He is in the process of conforming us to Himself.

The days ahead may be difficult, yet take courage the Lord has overcome the world. He is not done with you and is just starting to use you. The Lord wants to do great and mighty things in and through you. Keep looking up, see Him work through you to flourish you in troubling times for His greater good.

About Compass

Compass - finances God's way is a global, non-denominational movement teaching financial discipleship and generosity. The purpose is to serve churches, businesses, ministries, schools and other organisations by providing biblically based solutions on handling money and possessions.

Our vision is to see everyone, everywhere faithfully living by God's financial principles in all areas of their lives.

Compass' mission is to help people everywhere to learn, apply and teach Gods financial and business principles. We are looking for three major outcomes.
• To know Christ more intimately as we trust and obey Him, experiencing Christ at work.
• To become free from worry, fear, stress and anxiety and then be free to serve and love the Lord and our neighbours.
• To contribute to fulfilling the Great Commission by giving our money and other resources to fund the work of the Church.

The Compass Global Team is comprised of local leadership on 6 continents – Europe, Asia, South America, North America, Africa and the Indian sub-continent. Our continental offices serve more than 90 nations around the world.

To get in touch, please visit the Compass Global landing page www. compass1.global

Resources

Compass has developed a wide range of resources in a wide variety of formats, such as DVD based teaching, workshops, small group studies, e-books and online learning.

There are teaching resources for all ages, from small children through students to adults; with application to areas of life such as business, church, marriage and family.

Compass has resources in many languages.

Contact our European continental offices at www.compass1.eu